Practitioner Series

D1317943

Springer

London
Berlin
Heidelberg
New York
Hong Kong
Milan
Paris
Santa Clara
Singapore
Tokyo

Other titles in this series:

The Project Management Paradigm
K. Burnett
3-540-76238-8

Electronic Commerce and Business Communications
M. Chesher and R. Kaura
3-540-19930-6

Key Java
J. Hunt and A. McManus
3-540-76259-0

The Politics of Usability
L. Trenner and J. Bawa
3-540-76181-0

Distributed Applications Engineering
I. Wijegunaratne and G. Fernandez
3-540-76210-8

Finance for IT Decision Makers
M. Blackstaff
3-540-76232-9

Conceptual Modeling for User Interface Development
D. Benyon, T. Green and D. Bental
1-85233-009-0

The Renaissance of Legacy Systems
I. Warren
1-85233-060-0

Java for Practitioners
J. Hunt
1-85233-093-7

Daniel Serain

Middleware

Translator: Iain Craig

Springer

Daniel Serain
Digital Equipment Corporation
Centre Technique Europe
B.P. 027 - 950, route des Colles
06901 Sophia-Antipolis Cedex France

Translator
Dr Iain Craig
Department of Computer Science, University of Warwick
Coventry CV4 7AL, UK

ISBN 1-85233-011-2 Springer-Verlag London Berlin Heidelberg

British Library Cataloguing in Publication Data
Serain, Daniel
    Middleware. – (Practitioner Seriers)
    1.Middleware
    I.Title
    004.3'6
    ISBN 1852330112

Library of Congress Cataloging-in-Publication Data
Serain, Daniel, 1947–
    [Middleware. English]
    Middleware / Daniel Serain ; translator, Iain Craig.
        p.   cm. –– (Practitioner series)
    Translation of: Le middleware.
    Includes bibliographic references and index.
    ISBN 1-85233-011-2 (alk. paper)
    1. Middleware.   I. Title.   II. Series: Practitioner series
(Springer-Verlag)
QA76.76.M54S4713   1999
005.7'13––dc21   98–49412

Le Middleware. Concepts et technologies
© Masson, Paris, 1997
2nd Edition: Middleware et Internet. CORBA, COM/DCOM, JavaRMI et ActiveX
© Dunod 1999

© Springer-Verlag London Limited 1999
Printed in Great Britain

Typesetting: Elaine Bingham, 30 Wentworth Road, Dronfield, UK
Printed and bound at the Athenæum Press Ltd, Gateshead, Tyne and Wear, UK
34/3830-543210 Printed on acid-free paper

Contents

Foreword vii

Acknowledgements ix

1. Middleware 1
   1.1 The Problems to Be Solved 1
   1.2 Middleware 4
   1.3 Internet and Client–Server Architectures 24
   1.4 Object-oriented Modelling (OOM) 27
   1.5 Conclusions 29

2. Message-based Middleware 31
   2.1 Introduction 31
   2.2 Principal Functions 32
   2.3 Evaluation of the Principal Products 38

3. RPC-based Middleware 43
   3.1 The Client–Server Model 43
   3.2 Client–Server and Procedure Call 44
   3.3 Principles of the Remote Procedure Call Architecture 46
   3.4 Concept of Contract between Client and Server 47
   3.5 Structure of Communication 51
   3.6 The Standard 54

4. CORBA: Standard Object-based Middleware 63
   4.1 Introduction 63
   4.2 The CORBA Conceptual Model 66
   4.3 The CORBA Architecture 70
   4.4 The CORBA 2.0 Standard 75
   4.5 Object Services 78

5. OLE/COM: Object-based Middleware from Microsoft 81
   5.1 Introduction 81
   5.2 The COM Object Model 82
   5.3 OLE2 92

6. Comparison between CORBA and OLE/COM 97
   6.1   Introduction 97
   6.2   Code Reuse: Inheritance and Aggregation 99
   6.3   Composite Document Handling:
        OLE2 (COM) and OpenDoc (CORBA) 101
   6.4   Bridge between CORBA and DCOM 103
   6.5   Summary Table 104

7. Internet and Middleware 105
   7.1   Introduction to the Internet 105
   7.2   Internet Architectures 118
   7.3   Putting an Application onto the Internet 122

8. JAVA RMI and Java Beans 131
   8.1   The Java Language 131
   8.2   Distributed Processing with Java 133
   8.3   Internet: Downloading and Execution of Applets 135
   8.4   Remote Method Invocation: Java RMI 140
   8.5   Java Beans and ActiveX 144

9. Introduction to Object Technology 149
   9.1   The Concept of an Object 149
   9.2   Principal Characteristics of Object Technology 151

**10. MethodF™: A Method for Object-oriented Analysis
    and Design** 165
   10.1 Introduction 165
   10.2 Specification Phase 168
   10.3 Analysis Phase 174
   10.4 Design Phase 187
   10.5 Implementation Phase 193
   10.6 Summary of MethodF's Principal Steps 199

11. Conclusion 201
   11.1 Choosing Middleware 202
   11.2 The Complete Approach: From Company
        Requirements to Middleware Infrastructure 203

Bibliography/Cybography 205

Glossary 207

Index 211

Foreword

Historically, middleware has existed since the end of the 1960s. Recently, this term appeared in the literature following the emergence of client–server architectures and as a response to the requirement to integrate software running in a heterogenous environment.

Middleware is a layer of software positioned between the operating system and applications, allowing the exchange of information between them. It forms the infrastructure of an information system on which the software needs to be connected. It appears, thus, as the structuring element required in every complex system architecture.

M. Jean-Claude Grattarola, Maître de Conférence at the University of Nice, Sophia Antipolis, always careful to assist students towards a better understanding of the business world, recognized the importance of this set of technologies for the design of information systems and allowed them to be taught in the third year of the Institut Professionnalisé MIAGE (Méthodes Informatiques Appliquées à la Gestion des Entreprises). This book represents the supporting text of the course which I have the pleasure of giving.

This book is aimed at two categories of reader. The first category groups together people who, for their work and their duties in a company, are interested in information systems. These persons, without necessarily being computer scientists, know what is at stake in industry. The second category of reader is represented by people who want to know more about middleware technology and associated design methodology. Students belong to this category.

The first chapter forms a summary of the book and it is particularly aimed at readers belonging to the first category. It begins with typical problems encountered in companies which can be solved by an approach based on middleware technologies. The description of these technologies requires no deep technical knowledge. The tight overlapping of the Internet and middleware is presented. Then, every architectural approach implies a development methodology. This forms the structure which rests on middleware technologies and which ends in the satisfaction of users' needs.

The other chapters return in detail to each of the technologies: message-based middleware, RPC-based middleware and object-based middleware, the client–server model and Internet, Java and object modelling. The descriptions are much more technical here, but nevertheless sufficiently tutorial in nature to be understood by someone who is not an expert.

The concluding chapter provides the criteria which must be taken into account to choose the middleware technology which best suits the needs of the company.

The importance of the role played by middleware in the design of complex information systems is not yet sufficiently understood. This set of technologies has, however, become essential for the implementation of future systems. The aim of this book is to contribute to its promulgation and its understanding.

D. Serain

Acknowledgements

I wish to express my thanks to:

- M. Jean-Claude Grattarola, Maître de Conférence at the University of Nice, Sophia Antipolis, without whom this book would never have been written. This book is closely connected with the course which I teach at MIAGE at his invitation.

- Mme S. Ghernaouti-Hélie, Professor at the Ecole des HEC, University of Lausanne, for her enthusiastic help during the entire process of editing this book.

- M. Laurent-David Charbit, manager at Michelin USA, who, with his real-life experience of problems in business information technology and his interest in new technology, has given me hope that this book is also useful to managers in industry.

- M. Martin Malina, Director at Digital Equipment Corporation, who knew how to create an environment ripe for the acquisition and dissemination of the knowledge contained in this book.

1. Middleware

This chapter studies client–server architectures which satisfy the current major needs of the industry and which rest on the unifying concept of the software communications bus. This bus, invisible to the users of information systems, makes the exchange of information between applications easy. It is realized using new software technologies which form middleware. These middleware technologies lead to the concepts of application interface, distributed application, encapsulation of an existing application, management of distributed applications, client–server model and the Internet. The goal of this chapter is to demonstrate the importance of middleware and to introduce all the concepts mentioned above and position them with respect to each other. Each of them is studied in the ensuing chapters.

1.1 The Problems to Be Solved

In order to develop and to be competitive, every company must continually adapt to the needs and constraints of the market. This situation leads it to define objectives which will be achieved thanks to new working methods which appeal to the use of information tools. New software must be bought or developed, old applications must be modified. All software, whatever its origin, must be able to exchange information. On the other hand, in order to be ever closer to the client, a company must make its software accessible to any location in the world.

Thus every company's data processing (DP) manager sees themselves confronted, at the software level, with three main types of problem:

1. the integration of software from different sources;

2. access to software inside or outside the company;

3. rapid application development.

Rapid application development does not constitute the subject matter of this book. However, the architectures and the technologies of concern contribute strongly to the acceleration of the development of applications. We will concentrate therefore on the first two types of problem.

1.1.1 Integration of Applications

The dream of every DP manager is to be able to easily develop their environment. Now the introduction of new software implies that they can exchange data with existing software. Communication links must be constructed between each pair of applications which have to communicate. These links can be complex and hard to manage if the two applications which are inter-communicating run on different machines.

In the example shown in Figure 1.1, the applications A and B must be able to communicate. Let us assume that application A is old and stores its data in a local file F. Let us make the assumption that the new application, B, obtains its data through reading file F1 whose format is different from that of file F. Let us also assume that applications A and B operate on different machines. The creation of a communications link between these two applications implies the use of transfer software and the change of data format from that used in file F to that used in file F1.

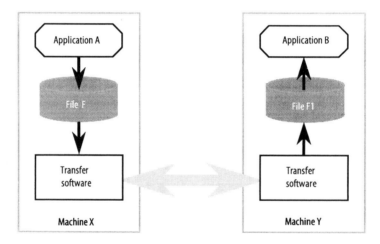

Fig 1.1 Simple communication link between two applications.

Note that the assumptions made in the previous example are highly realistic. In order to profit from the capacities of new generations of machine, much more software is designed to run on them. Existing software, the average age of which is 12 years, runs on machines of the previous generation whose operating systems are generally non-standard (or are proprietary).

Very often, to acquire software useful to their company, a DP manager is led to buying a new machine. It comes about that their information environment becomes heterogeneous and thus more complex to manage.

Over the course of many years, applications have been added to the information systems of many companies with the result that, if we look at them carefully, their internal communications organization closely resembles a bowl of spaghetti (Fig 1.2). Such a system is difficult to manage and to evolve. In order to avoid ending up with an inextricable system of inter-application connections, a global solution must be envisaged. This solution must suggest a new architecture which allows the easy integration of new applications and the adaptation of existing applications.

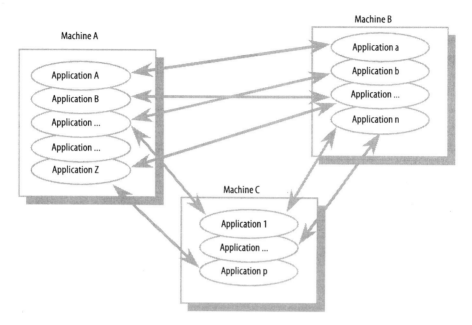

Fig 1.2 Example of a spaghetti system.

1.1.2 Availability of Applications in the Whole World

A number of factors combine to allow access to a company's software, both from inside the organization and from outside. Let us consider some examples:

- Ever tighter relations between clients and providers leading the latter to give their clients free access to their ordering system. Clients can thus browse through the list of products and prices and make their orders direct.

- In a banking setting, clients are apt to travel around the whole world and to appeal to services from their bank. The possession of a private telecommunications network for a company represents a high cost and thus a brake on its geographical development.

- Companies having many branches must maintain a certain number of applications and connect them to the central site. The maintenance of the software at the same version level in all divisions constitutes an incompletely solved problem.

At the present time, companies feel the need to increase their geographical presence by offering easy access to their applications and at the lowest possible cost.

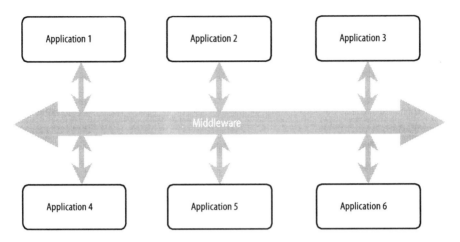

Fig 1.3 Middleware or communications bus for distributed applications.

1.2 Middleware

The first goal of the middleware technologies is to solve the problem of the integration of software. We have seen in section 1.1.1 that the addition of an application to an information system which consists of n, can lead to the construction of n communications links and $2n$ application interfaces. One way of solving this problem is to introduce the concept of a unique communications bus or middleware, to which applications connect through the intermediary of a clearly defined interface. The result of such an approach is depicted in Figure 1.3. It can be seen that all the connections are grouped into a single data exchange system.

Such an architecture leaves one to assume that the communications bus (or middleware) which permits the exchange of data between two or more applications offers a certain number of services.

We can mention:

- The availability of middleware on different machines. The information system of every company is heterogeneous, that is, it is composed of machines of different marks and types. Applications running on these machines must be able to communicate.

- The reliability of transfer. When the sending application hands a message to the middleware, it must be assured that the destination will receive it once and once only. This must be the case even when the network or a machine crashes.

- Adaptation to traffic. The bandwidth of the communications bus must be able to sustain an increase in traffic due to the addition of applications. The capacity of middleware to adapt to changes (variation in the number of applications, number and type of machines) is elemental since it forms every application system skeleton.

- The diversity of communication structures. An application can wish to communicate with a single other application or to send the same message to n destinations. In this last case, it is desirable that the sender can put a single copy of the message on the bus and that the bus is responsible for sending it to all designated destinations.

- The use of a name. The sending application of a message denotes the destination not by its physical address, but by its name. It is up to the transmission system to convert this name to a physical address. This service allows the transfer of an application from one machine to another with no consequence for the applications which communicate with it.

- The concept of transaction. The concept of transaction specifies that if several entities (e.g., applications) belong to a single transaction, all of them must be able to execute their work or none of them can. Let us assume, for example, that to make travel arrangments, an agency uses two applications. The first application supports the reservation of the flights and the second supports hotel reservations. It can be assumed that if we cannot reserve a flight for a given destination, it is useless to reserve a hotel there. In the same way, travellers do not want to find themselves in a town if they have no hotel room. Thus the transaction which here represents a journey will only be realized if the requests for flights and hotels are satisfied. If one or other of them is not, no reservation is performed and the transaction which represents the trip is nul.

Positioning of Middleware

Middleware forms a communications structure that is independent of the machines' operating systems and of the nature of the transmission network being used. In the OSI model which defines the different levels of communication between information systems, middleware is situated at the very top. It defines the communications protocol for use between applications.

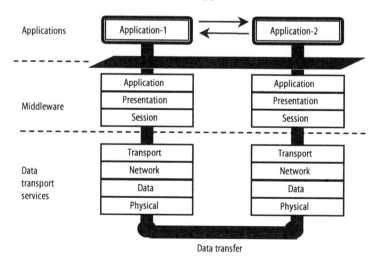

Fig 1.4 Location of middleware in the OSI model.

This inter-application communications structure rests on the communications structures at lower levels such as network protocols (TCP/IP, DECnet, SNA or OSI) and/or the mechanisms offered by the operating systems (e.g., interrupt processing).

1.2.1 The Client–Server Model

While several entities must communicate among themselves, a communications protocol must be defined and accepted by everyone in order to avoid confusion. Different communication schemes exist. Television provides us with numerous examples: a debate run by an arbiter (a journalist) who gives the floor in turn (or according to some complex algorithm) to the participants; a face-to-face discussion between two people – of these, one is the interviewer and the other is the interviewee. The goal of these structures is that each question receives a reply, and that the question is settled.

Fig 1.5 The master/pupil relation represents a particular communication structure.

Over the years, different communications structures have been used to allow the exchange of data between programs. One of them emerged because of its flexibility. It is based on the interviewer/interviewee model and is characterized as follows:

- Communications imply only two entities. This model assumes that every communication concerning the members of a group can be decomposed into a set of exchanges between two members.

- One entity has the initiative in the dialogue (the interviewer) and the other is waiting for a request (the interviewee).

- The interviewee entity is programmed to reply to a very precise set of requests.[1] The list of authorized requests must be perfectly defined. This list is called the interviewed entity's interface.

---

[1] Here is where the analogy with television ends.

In this communication model, the interviewed entity is described as offering services. For each request there is a corresponding well-defined service. For this reason, this entity is also called the *server*. The other entity which requires the services is therefore called the *client*. The set forms the client–server model.

The operation of the client–server model of communications is as follows:

- The client sends a message containing a request to the server.

- The server executes the service associated with the request sent by the client.

- The server returns to the client a message containing the result of the service that has been performed.

In this model, communications are always initiated by the client. The server is in a reactive mode. The model does not bother itself with the way in which communications are actually performed. It only assumes that there exists a means to exchange messages. The interface to the server appears as an essential element in the communications. It describes the permitted requests. Figure 1.6 depicts the client–server model.

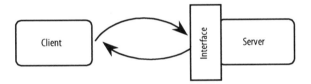

Fig 1.6 The client–server model.

1.2.2 The Three-Tier Client–Server Model

At this stage, it is interesting to see how the client–server model can be concretely applied. A first possibility consists of defining a client–server relationship between two applications. A second possibility consists of decomposing an application into a set of elements that are connected by this relation. Let us see how.

The functional analysis of an application reveals three parts:

1. The user interface part. It is most often graphical (windows) and allows the user to talk to the application. Very often this part must be able to operate on different types of machines: PC, Macintosh, workstations or dumb terminals. This component is called the *graphical user interface* or *user service* (in Microsoft terminology).

2. The part which actually does the processing. It contains the logic of the application representing the rules of the company. This component is called the *processing server* or *business server* (in Microsoft terminology).

3. The part which accesses the data. This part contains the procedures which access the data. It knows, therefore, the structure of the database(s). This component is called the *data server*.

An application based on the client–server model and constructed from these three components leads to a model called the three-tier client–server model, each stage only communicating with its immediate neighbours (see Fig 1.7):

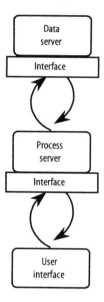

Fig 1.7 The three-tier application model.

- The ground floor is composed of the graphical user interface. It is the entry point into the application.
- The first floor is composed of the processing server.
- A client–server relation exists between the graphical user interface which plays the role of a client and the processing server which plays the part of the server.
- In order to be a server, the processing part must possess a perfectly defined interface which describes what is on offer.
- The data server forms the second floor.
- A client–server relation exists between the processing server which plays the part of client and the data server which plays the part of the server.
- In order to be a server, the data server must possess a perfectly defined interface which describes the services which provide access to the data.

It can be noted that the part which acts as the processing server plays two roles: as a server with reference to the graphical user interface and that of client with respect to the data server.

The decomposition of an application into the three parts described above presents numerous advantages:

- Each part is physically independent of the others. Thus, the three stages can operate on three different machines, communications between the stages can be performed by middleware.

- Programming and maintenance of each of the stages can be performed independently of the other stages as long as the interface does not change.

- Functional separation leads to making the central code of the application (the processing server) independent of the structure and the location of the data. It is also independent of the way in which the data are provided by the user.

At this stage, it is interesting to examine the middleware technologies which allow the implementation of the client–server model as well as the integration of distributed applications.

1.2.3 Message-based Middleware

Message-based middleware was one of the first technologies to implement the concept of a communications bus that is common to several applications and which lets them exchange messages. The interesting thing about this approach was also that it simplifies programming by allowing the programmer to avoid the network protocols level or calls to functions provided by the operating system.

Several products using this concept have been available on the market for some years. They have a considerable level of maturity and form a highly reliable technology. They are often used in information systems for industrial manufacture. For example, BMW uses the product DECmessageQ from Digital Equipment in order to handle their assembly lines. IBM has also proposed a message-based middleware product called MQSeries.

Principal Characteristics

The message-based technology is characterized by the fact that it is not standardized. The best way in which we can give the main characteristics is thus to examine one of the more advanced products. If we refer to DECmessageQ, the following functions are available:

- Asynchronous transmission of messages. DECmessageQ allows applications to communicate in independent or interdependent ways. The asynchronous message exchange mechanism allows the sending application (the client) to put its message into a message queue and continue with its processing. The receiving application (the server), when it is available, reads the message and processes it. Thus, client and server operate in their own rhythm. In the synchronous communications mode, when the client has placed its message into the server's input queue, it must wait for the reply. No parallel processing by the client or server is possible.

- Guaranteed delivery of messages. DECmessageQ allows the client to label a message in order to guarantee its delivery. Each message thus marked, is copied to disk so as not to be lost. There it remains until the original has arrived at the destination. In the case of a system crash, network or server failure, the middleware re-transmits the message automatically until the server receives it. It is only then that the copy on disk is deleted. This system does not predict when the message will be processed by the server but it guarantees that it will be.

- Availability on a number of platforms.[2] The DECmessageQ product is available on about 20 platforms. These include the Windows-NT, UNIX (AIX, HP-UX, Sun), OVMS, IBM MVS, etc. Because no standards exist, message-based middleware products cannot be used together. It is therefore important that a product runs on several platforms in order to suit the needs of the users.

- Selective reading of messages. DECmessageQ allows servers to read messages not in arrival order but in an order determined by the sender, the priority level of the message, or its type and its class. They are defined by the user in order to identify the contents or the aim of the message.

- Broadcasting of messages. The DECmessageQ software allows a client to send one message simultaneously to a group of servers with a single operation. The receiving applications are those which have explicitly expressed the desire to receive such messages. Thus, the sender knows neither the number nor the location of the receivers. The fact that the sender and the distribution system are kept separate allows the latter to be changed without effect upon the code of the sender.

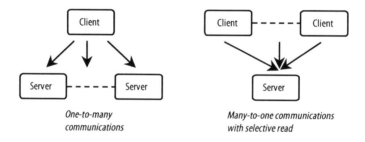

One-to-many
communications

Many-to-one communications
with selective read

Fig 1.8 Examples of communication structures.

Advantages

- One of the advantages that today determines message-based middleware is its great reliability. Existing products have enough maturity to be used in applications that are essential to the correct functioning of a company.

- A second advantage is due to the fact that this technology uses traditional programming techniques. In particular, it does not appeal to the latest object-

---

[2] Here the term "platform" means a machine and its operating system. Thus an Intel machine equipped with the Windows-NT operating system is considered to be a different platform from the same Intel machine equipped with the UNIX operating system.

oriented programming techniques. This is important because the implementation of message-based software implies an action by a programmer at the level of the code of the communicating applications.

Disadvantages

- The message-based technology imposes no restrictions on message structure; they must be constructed by the application which sends them and must be understood by the receiving application. This means that the client application must possess code to construct the message and that the server application must have code to decode it. The code of each application contains the code needed to connect to the communication system (see Fig 1.9). This is not considered elegant from the architectural viewpoint, because every modification to the communications system affects the application itself and the application programmer must also know the communication system. This knowledge represents a non-negligible expertise. For example, certain types of data are not represented in the same way on different platforms.[3] Current middleware products only perform limited encoding and this job remains in the hands of the application programmer.

- There are no standards for this technology. This means that a user cannot combine two middleware products from two different vendors. It is also not possible to create messages using a standard format in the hope that they will be portable across different middleware products. All of this implies that a user must choose a product and stick to it. This choice is important because middleware represents the infrastructure of the information system and cannot easily be replaced.

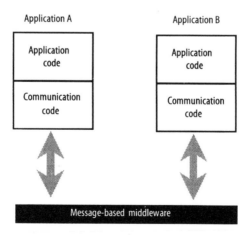

Fig 1.9 Using message queues, applications contain code for communications.

---

[3] There exist, for example, two standards for coding character strings: ASCII and EBCDIC. The exchange of character strings between two platforms each using only one of the standards imposes a format conversion in both directions.

Bridges between products are, however, starting to appear. Thus, version 3.2 of DECmessageQ from the Digital Equipment Corporation offers a certain level of interoperability with the MQSeries product from IBM. Additionally, the makers of such software have formed an association[4] in order to promote this technology and to define standards. The pressure of progress not being very strong, it can be thought that the definition and implementation of standards will take a long time.

Future Developments

Message-based middleware is highly dynamic and offers, with each new version of the products, new functions. In order to show this tendency, here are the principal functions which will be offered in the next version (V4.0) of DECmessageQ:

- Self-describing messages. This function includes in the message all elements which allow its interpretation. It allows the design of applications which have to communicate without having precisely defined the structure of the messages to be exchanged. For example, the sender of a message can add the date to an existing message, or change its length, without consequences as far as the code in the receiving application is concerned, if it does not use the added data. This system also translates the data from one format to another when the exchange takes place between different platform types.

  This new function illustrates the tendency towards simplifying the life of the application designer, to increasing the flexibility of the communications system and to progressively integrating all the appropriate functions.

- Name system. This system allows messages to designate the receiver not only by the number of its message queue, but also by a name.

- Very large messages. The maximum size of messages that are transferred is increased to 4 Mb. This simplifies the exchange of complete files between applications.

Conclusions

Message-based middleware offers systems designers a simple, flexible, asynchronous, reliable, high-performance tool which enables the current problem of integrating existing applications to be resolved. However, the absence of a standard and the fact that application code must contain communications code has led certain groups to reflect on other ways to construct and integrate applications.

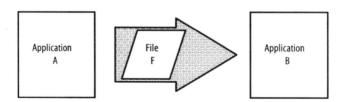

Fig 1.10 Entire files can be exchanged between applications thanks to the maximum message size of 4 Mb.

[4] The Message-Oriented Middleware Association (MOMA).

1.2.4 Middleware Based on Remote Procedure Calls

Message-based middleware has, as its first aim, the integration of existing applications. When a new application is designed, and when it is desired to distribute it on several platforms, the question is raised as to the unit of distribution. With message-based middleware, the unit of distribution is the application itself. When it is desired to decompose an application into distributable elements, it remains to define the characteristics of these elements. Their "size" must represent a consequent processing time with respect to the transmission of the request which requires its execution. This "size" represents the level of granularity of the distributed entity.

If one refers to the existing elements of programming, the concept of procedure (or function) appears a good candidate for distribution. This concept is known and understood by everyone and represents a functional entity which is quite precise and whose interface is perfectly defined.

In traditional programming, every application is composed of a body of the main program and a set of procedures (see Fig 1.11). The client–server model applies perfectly to this scheme. The main program which calls the procedures appears as the client to each one of them, and the server is composed of the set of procedures. Each procedure offers a service and the server is composed of the set of these services. The interface of a service is exactly the interface of a procedure, that is its name and the set of its parameters. The interface of the server is formed of the set of the interfaces of the procedures which it contains.

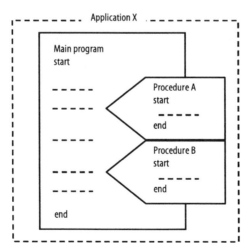

Fig 1.11 An application is composed of a main program and a set of procedures.

This approach demonstrates the importance of the server. This latter is perfectly defined. Our goal is, however, to make this set of procedures (the server) totally independent of the main program (the client). This independence clearly authorizes other clients to appeal to the services of the server. These other clients are not forced to be written in the same language as the server and can, however, communicate with it. This leads to the description of the interface of the server in a language that is independent of the programming languages of the clients and the servers. This language is called IDL (Interface Definition Language).

In this model of distributed procedures, the client calls the procedures which compose the server as if they were local to the client. In fact, they can be situated on any machine on the network (Fig 1.12). The middleware which allows this communication between client and server is called *remote procedure call middleware* (RPC middleware).

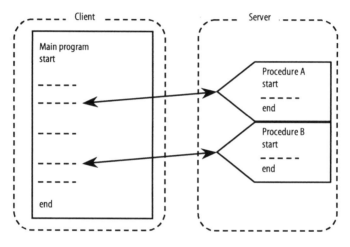

Fig 1.12 The client-server model applied to distributed procedures.

At the level of the client, nothing differentiates between the call of a remote procedure and the call of a local one. This means that the code that prepares the request, which is necessary, is external to the client. In message-based middleware, this code forms an integral part of the client and must, therefore, be written by the application programmer. Here, this piece of code is automatically generated by the IDL language which describes the interface presented by the server used by the client (see Fig 1.13). The piece of code associated with the client is called a *client stub*, and that associated with the server is called the *server stub*.

Primary Characteristics

The RPC middleware technology can be characterized as follows:

- Code in the client and in the server is independent of the communications system. The client does not know whether the procedure is local or remote.

- Code in the client does not have to prepare the message, nor to locate the server. This work is done by the RPC middleware stub.

- The dialogue system is entirely external to the client and server. It is described in a specific language called IDL in which the code necessary for communication is automatically generated.

- The communication structure is constructed at compilation time. It is therefore completely defined before execution commences.

- Communications are synchronous. After having called the procedure the client program waits for the result. It is only when the result is returned to it that it resumes its processing.

- The RPC technology is entirely standardized. The standardization includes the IDL language as well as all the services necessary for communication.

- Nowadays, many vendors offer products which conform to the standards. From this fact, it is possible to combine different products.

RPC technology exists today on very stable products. However, its success is not as assured as that of message-based middleware. Its basic principle, the procedure call, seems to be at too low a level. During the design of complex information systems, the aspects of distribution must be taken into account very early in the design phase. Now, the concept of procedure only appears very late in the design phase. The use of RPC middleware as a distribution system implies the modification of current analysis and design methods by introducing the concept of the server at the highest level possible.

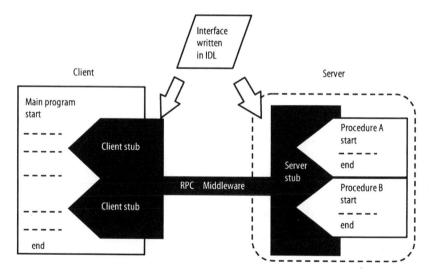

Fig 1.13 In RPC middleware, communications code is automatically generated.

If we compare the characteristics of RPC technology with that required of a communications bus (see section 1.2), it can be seen that this technology offers everything except the following:

- Reliability of transfer. If for any reason the server or the network do not work, the message will not be delivered and will be lost. The handling of errors or crashes is left entirely in the hands of the client code.

- The concept of transaction. The current RPC technology does not offer integrity of a transaction. This is a very serious limitation and for this reason, some software vendors offer non-standard products, based on RPC, which implement the concept of a transaction.

- Transmission of messages. The communications organization in RPC is one-to-one and not one-to-many. This means that a client can only talk to one server at a time during a request.

The RPC technology is available through products of many manufacturers thanks to the existence of a standard called OSF DCE (Open Software Foundation Distributed Computing Environment). Among the other middleware technologies, it represents the lowest level communications layer.

1.2.5 Object-oriented Middleware: CORBA and COM

RPC middleware uses, as its distribution unit, the concept of procedure. This programming concept does not, unfortunately, exist at the level of analysis methods, that is, at the level of modelling. This limitation has led people to reflect on the identification of an entity which will be of a sufficiently high level to be considered during the modelling phases and to be sufficiently close to programming concepts to be translated easily into a programming language. Such an entity exists. It provides a language which is common to the domains of the user and computer person. It is called an *object*.

Briefly,[5] an object has a name, has attributes to define its state, and operations to describe its behaviour. Objects belong to the world as it currently is. Thus, for example, a bank account can be considered as an object. Its number is its name, its possible attributes can be its balance and currency in which it is expressed. Its operations are: open, deposit, withdraw, enquire or close the account. The use of object technology allows one to model complex information applications by combining objects using a range of static and/or dynamic relations. In this way, an application appears as a set of co-operating objects (Fig 1.14). From this fact, the object constitutes a completely suitable unit of distribution.

Object technology has very interesting properties. In particular:

- The concept of encapsulation. This concept allows us to separate the external aspects of an object forming its interface (names of the attributes and of the operations), from the internal aspects (way in which its attributes and operations are implemented). The external aspect is defined during the modelling phase and the internal one is made precise during programming. This concept allows us to speak of an object without bothering about the way in which it is implemented.

- An object system appears as a list of interfaces behind which is found the code associated with the attributes and operations. It is thus possible to modify the code independent of the interfaces. This forms a fundamental aspect of object technology.

---

[5] Chapter 9 discusses object technology in detail.

- The concept of inheritance. An object can inherit characteristics (attributes and operations) from another object. This mechanism makes the model more precise and eases the reuse of software.

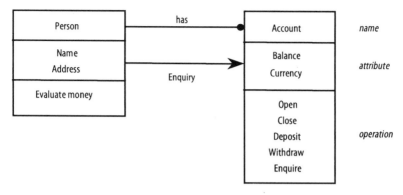

Fig 1.14 Example of an application composed of two objects, Person and Account.

If we assume that objects are distributed across a network, inter-object communication corresponds to a request made by one object (the client) to execute an operation on another object (the server). This request is performed using a specific communications bus called *object middleware* or an *Object Request Broker* (ORB).

This model offers functions similar to RPC. The client object does not know the location of the server object, and the client does not have to construct the request message.

Communication between client and server objects can be defined in a static or dynamic fashion:

- Static communication is performed in the same way as with RPC technology. This communication is described in an IDL language which is standardized and object oriented, called CORBA IDL (Common Object Request Broker Architecture Interface Definition Language). Client and server stubs are constructed from the CORBA IDL code which allows the connection of the client and server objects, respectively, to the middleware object.

- Dynamic communication is established by the client when it executes. The client can interrogate the middleware object in order to know the interfaces of the objects available across the network. The server for the selected interface has no way of knowing if the request which it receives was produced in a static or dynamic fashion.

The middleware object exemplifies the concept of an interface possessing the following characteristics:

- An interface represents the services offered by the server object. These services are in fact directly associated with the object's operations.

- It supports the generation of new interfaces using the inheritance mechanism. The infrastructure of an object-oriented information system is formed by the set of the interfaces connected to the communication bus. Their update is eased by the inheritance mechanism which allows the introduction of new things while allowing old ones to be retained.

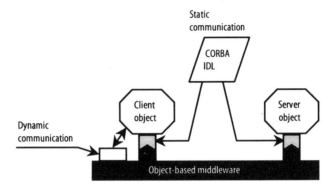

Fig 1.15 Object-based middleware allows communications established in a static fashion.

- An interface can be associated with one or more servers. Recall that an interface describes a set of services but does not specify how and by whom these services are performed. This decoupling between description of the service and the service itself allows:

  o Several implementations to be offered by a single service. Thus no constraint is imposed on the server itself. In particular, it does not even need to be written in an object-oriented language.

  o Connection of a server with several interfaces. A service offered by a server can figure in different interfaces. Rather than duplicate the server code, the latter can be activated by its different interfaces.

  o Conversion of an existing application into a server. To do this, it is enough to connect it to an object interface one of whose services this application can provide. This approach allows the painless transformation of an application environment into an object environment.

A New Vision of Information Systems

The set of interfaces of the objects existing in an information system represent the services offered by such a system. This leads to a new view of an information system. It is no longer described as a set of applications, but as offering a set of services (Fig 1.16). The great interest in object-based middleware is that it contains a database containing the list of all available interfaces. It is therefore possible, at any time, to consult this list in order to know the capacities of the system. Every client object can consult it and discover the new services dynamically.

In such an environment, the addition of software simply requires the introduction of one or a few interfaces describing the services offered by this new software and the attachment of them to these interfaces. If this software must access existing services, communication with these services must be described in the CORBA IDL language.

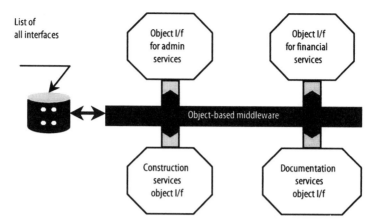

Fig 1.16 A new approach: an information system is described by the list of offered services.

Standards and Object-based Middleware

In distributed object-based middleware, two models coexist. The first model has been around since 1990, and was established as the international standard by the Object Management Group (OMG).[6] It has the name CORBA (Common Object Request Broker Architecture). The second model was proposed by Microsoft and is called DCOM (Distributed Component Object Model).

Several products implement CORBA middleware. ObjectBroker from Digital Equipment Corporation,[7] DSOM (Distributed Systems Object Model) from IBM, DOE (Distributed Objects Everywhere) from Sun, and ORBPlus from Hewlett-Packard can be mentioned. Some of these products have become relatively mature thanks to their availability since the start of the 1990s.

The Microsoft product is more recent (1996). Beyond Windows platforms, it also runs on UNIX machines. Thus, Microsoft's DCOM model tends to be positioned as an alternative to the CORBA model.

From the above, it seems that the CORBA model runs on all major platforms, the PC-based Windows world included, but the latter is dominated by the Microsoft object model. So, all the software from this company is based on the Component Object Model (COM), which recently became a distributed model. In order to allow the CORBA and COM worlds to communicate, specifications are currently being produced by OMG.

---

[6] Several hundred companies are members of this organization and participate in the creation of standards.

[7] This technology now belongs to BEA Systems Inc.

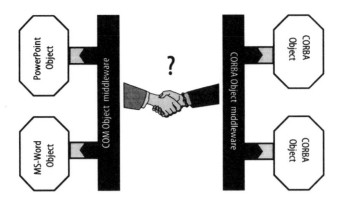

Fig 1.17 Object-based middleware is divided into two worlds. Will they understand each other?

1.2.6 Current Limitations of Middleware Technology

Three main middleware technologies exist. They are: message-based, RPC, and distributed object-based middleware. They are differentiated by the nature of the distributed entities, and by the functions which they offer. Their existence is not due to a conscious decision, but are responses to industrial needs which ensure their success. All three are evolving very rapidly because the needs which they satisfy generate new ones. Thus their use shows the need to develop additional functions following the two principal axes:

- Resource handling. Middleware technologies do not offer them or only offer them on a highly limited basis:

  o Load balancing. If a server is unable to satisfy all requests, the middleware must be sufficiently intelligent to send them to an equivalent server.

  o Recovery in the case of error. If a server crashes, if the network is down, or if a machine has been halted, what will happen to the request? Some products ensure the delivery of the message but not in a definite time. This leads us to the concept of transaction.

- Transaction handling. A transaction is composed of a set of actions, all of which must be executed. If one of them fails, all of the other actions must be cancelled. A transaction is characterized by its:

  o Atomicity. A transaction represents an indivisible unit of work.

  o Consistency. At the end of the execution of a transaction, the system must again be in a stable state, for otherwise the transaction must be cancelled.

  o Independence. A transaction must not be affected by other transactions executing at the same time.

  o Duration. The results of a transaction are permanent.

It follows that a transaction forms the fundamental unit for recovery in the case of a crash, and consistency in a client–server system. The properties of a transaction are assured by the presence of a transaction monitor. This particular software handles:

- the two-phase commit protocol which ensures the atomicity of transactions and therefore the integrity of data;

- the routing of requests in the case of a crash of the network or of the server;

- the recovery when a failure has occurred – this ensures consistency of data when there is a cancellation of the transaction;

- the assurance that an action is executed once and once only;

- the starting and stopping of the servers;

- the execution flow of the transaction.

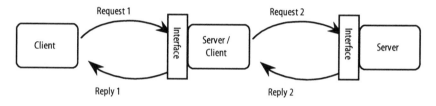

Transaction T = {Request 1 + Reply 1} + {Request 2 + Reply 2}

Fig 1.18 A transaction is a set of requests and their replies.

All the additional functions expected of middleware technology have been well understood for a very long time because they are also the requirements of some applications. These applications represent the tools which are indispensable to the execution of certain tasks. These are, for example, airline seat reservation, or bank account management applications. They are indispensable to the correct operation of companies, and have been, until now, implemented using specific software called transaction monitors which allow the sequential handling of transactions.[8]

Transaction systems traditionally used are centralized and require a powerful machine at the central site to which alphanumeric terminals (IBM 3270 or VT terminals) located in the branches are connected. The development of departmental information processing using PCs leads companies to integrate these two information worlds. The integration of software running on different machines imposes the use of transaction processing together with some kind of middleware technology. This problem has been formulated by the director of a software development company:

> "The problem today is to offer the integrity of a transaction in an environment composed of distributed and heterogenous machines (PCs and servers) using the client–server model."

At this stage the questions asked were:

---

[8] On-line transaction processing (OLTP).

- what are the different products and technologies which address this problem?

- do these products conform to the standards and do they operate on enough platforms?

1.2.6.1 Digital Reliable Transaction Router

In 1987, the Australian Stock Exchange undertook the complete replacement of its information system in order to be able to integrate different types of application and to use heterogenous platforms. At that time, no existing software matched their requirements. In order to meet this requirement Digital Equipment developed specific software called Digital Reliable Transaction Router (Digital RTR). This product offers a reliable infrastructure ensuring the continuous handling of software that is distributed using the client–server model. It also provides:

- assured message delivery;

- the concept of a transaction across a network – either WAN (Wide Area Network) or LAN (Local Area Network);

- a copy of the transaction in case of machine or network crash;

- a control system with highly complete tracing facilities;

- load balancing between different servers;

- distribution of large jobs and distribution of data.

Digital RTR implements a proprietary middleware system very similar to RPC. It operates on the major platforms currently on the market: UNIX (Alpha), Windows-NT, OpenVMS (VAX and Alpha).[9]

Digital RTR is incorporated in applications needing a high level of reliability. Its first users were mainly banks and financial institutions (stock companies). The Gartner Group (a computing consultancy which analyses products and advises on them) recommends this tool to those who are looking for a highly reliable infrastructure in order to construct their own OLTP system.

Digital RTR constitutes a very reliable and quite extensive middleware component. It uses a non-standard RPC technology because it was designed before the standards were finalized. This product has shown, by its numerous uses, the utility of the functions it offers.

1.2.6.2 ACMSxp

ACMSxp (a product from Digital Equipment Corporation) is a transaction monitor which allows the construction of applications requiring a high level of

---

[9] OpenVMS is an operating system running on VAX or Alpha machines. Alpha machines using a 64-bit processor, currently the fastest on the market, are able to execute more than a billion instructions per second.

reliability. This product demonstrates the current convergence of middleware tools and transaction monitors.

ACMSxp uses the services of RPC middleware and follows the OSF/DCE standard. It is very easy to use unlike other transaction monitors.

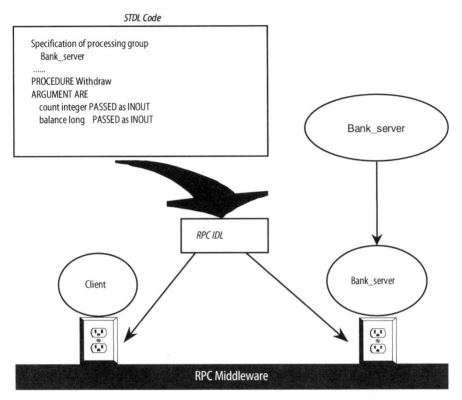

Fig 1.19 From SDTL code describing the transaction, the ACMSxp tool automatically generates RPC IDL code which, after compilation, generates client and server stubs.

ACMSxp offers:

- all the services of the standard OSF DCE technology: RPC, name servers, security and multi-threading;

- environment handling – this allows the verification of the state of all the components of the system (servers, network, etc.);

- the concept of transaction in a distributed environment;

- conformity with the STDL standard (Structured Transaction Definition Language) which allows the description of distributed transactions. This standard was adopted in March 1995.

ACMSxp is available on UNIX, Windows-NT and OpenVMS platforms. This tool suits the system designers who need a transaction monitor based on market standards.

1.2.6.3 Transaction Monitors and Standards

Transaction monitors represent the highest degree of sophistication in middleware. This translates into implementation complexity and in non-standard environments. However, the functions which transaction monitors offer are essential for some applications, but not for all. The market exists for middleware in its current form, as well as for transaction monitors. The latter must, in all cases, still develop because the applications which they manage are capable of being executed on different platforms with access to many different databases.

The only way to integrate this many disparate elements is to define standards specifying, for example, how a transaction monitor inter-operates with a resource manager, with other transaction monitors or with its servers. Unfortunately, the committee for the X/Open standard, which is very active in this area, does not seem to have had the time to take on all the other points of practical importance, such as name servers and security. Because these aspects are not formalized, the efficacy of the effort on standardization of transaction monitors will be illusory.

Today, the most reasonable approach is to limit oneself to a single transaction monitor operating on the widest range of platforms. For example, IBM suggests *"CICS on everything"*. This transaction monitor runs on MVS, AIX, UNIX (Alpha), HP-UX, OS/2, OS/400 and Windows-NT.

1.3 Internet and Client–Server Architectures

The middle of the 1990s saw the emergence of a new set of technologies called the *Internet*. The Internet represents a worldwide network of networks allowing computers which are connected to it to communicate between themselves. The Internet is interesting for the present study because it suggests a new way to support communication between entities previously called client and server.

At first, in order to familiarize ourselves with the Internet, we are going very briefly to describe its architecture (the Internet is described in more detail in Chapter 7). Next, we will see how it can be used in conjunction with middleware technologies to produce very powerful architectures.

1.3.1 Use of the Internet

The aspect of the Internet which interests us here is the World Wide Web (WWW). The World Wide Web is formed from an enormous set of multimedia documents distributed over some thousands of computers, and of a set of tools which allow one to access these documents. It allows access to multimedia documents, in particular alphanumeric ones, stored on a worldwide network of computers. To obtain access to these documents, the user must have a personal computer (typically a PC) and a connection to the telephone network. The computer must run a special program called a *browser*.

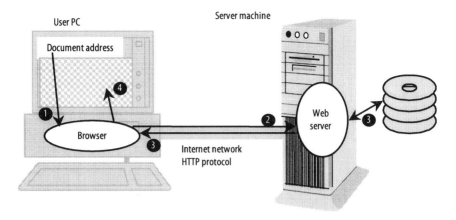

Fig 1.20 Use of the World Wide Web from a PC.

Each computer connected to the network and needing to appear as a document server must run a special piece of software called a Web server.

The World Wide Web operates as follows (see Fig 1.20):

1. The user, having activated the browser program, enters the address of a document.

2. The browser transmits the request to the network which knows how to locate the destination machine and sends it the name of the desired document. The protocol used on the network is called HTTP (HyperText Transfer Protocol). It is based on the standard network protocol TCP/IP (Transmission Control Protocol/Internet Protocol).

3. The Web server program finds the document on one of its disks and sends it to the machine which made the request.

4. When the document arrives, the browser processes it according to its type. If the type is alphanumeric, the document is displayed on the user's screen; if the type is audio, the sound is generated by the sound card on the PC, and so on.

The mechanism just described allows, quite simply, the transfer of files (or documents). But two important points already arise:

1. Access to the document can be made anywhere in the world. The only condition is the use of a telephone and computer.

2. Every alphanumeric document is displayed on the screen of the user's machine. In order to be "displayable" on any kind of machine, this document must be written in the standard language HTML (HyperText Markup Language). This document can contain fields to hold data and to display results. Thus nothing prevents this document from being the graphic interface to an application.

It is therefore possible to download that part of an application which consists of its user interface from anywhere in the world. In the three-tier client–server model introduced above, this part forms the graphical interface client part of the application. There remains, however, the matter of making it communicate with the rest of the application, that is with the processing server tier. In order to see how this is done, let us see another characteristic of the World Wide Web.

The Web Server

The Web server is a piece of software that is situated on a machine that is connected to the Internet and that can respond to user requests. The requests always refer to documents (or to files). The type of document dictates the action of the Web server. The server returns all the documents requested except those which have a program type. In this particular case, the Web server activates the program in question and passes to it the parameters the server has received from the client. When the program terminates, it gives the resulting data to the Web server which sends it back to the client.

In this mode of operation, the WWW allows the non-local execution of an application.

1.3.2 Architecture Combining Internet and Middleware Technologies

The mechanisms of the WWW allow the implementation of applications according to the client–server model. Let us consider the case of a two-tier application composed of a user interface tier and a processing server tier. Let us make the following assumptions:

- the interface code is written in the HTML language and is stored in a file of type alphanumeric, called *interface.html*;

- the processing server is already in an executable form and is stored in a file of type program (or binary), and is called *server.bin*.

The WWW allows us to execute this two-tier application on any machine and at any location. The mechanisms are the following:

1. Download the interface tier, that is, the *interface.html* file (see previous paragraph).

2. The browser displays the file *interface.html* on the user's screen. The latter has in front of them the interface to their application which is executing on their machine. It can then accept data and activate a request sent to the document *server.bin*, that is the processing server for the application.

3. This request circulates around the network and arrives at the Web server of the machine which has the requested file. This file containing a program is activated by the Web server by passing it the data which accompanies the request. Thus the server part of the application executes on the Web server's machine.

4. The results from the program, in HTML form, are returned to the client via the Web server.

5. The user's browser displays the results it has received.

This description shows the fact that the user PC can execute the client part (interface) of any application. Only this part of the application need be downloaded. In this approach, the HTTP protocol combined with the browser and the Web server seems like a particular type of middleware. The interesting thing about this approach can easily be appreciated. No application need reside on the PC. Their interface part can be downloaded on request. The resulting maintenance gains for applications is considerable.

In the case of applications built using the three-tier model, it is completely possible to use HTTP between the graphic interface and the processing server, and, between the latter and the data server, using either message-based, RPC or object-based middleware. Thus, in Figure 1.21, nothing stops us from having the three components of the application on three distinct machines.

The different possible architectures that are obtained by combining these technologies are described in detail in Chapter 7. They show the richness and the power of middleware technologies when they are combined over the Internet.

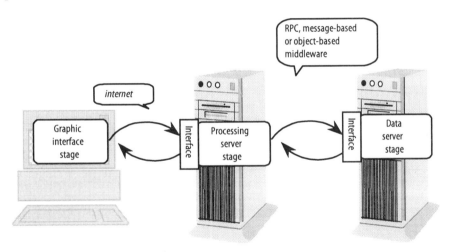

Fig 1.21 The three-tier client-server model allows the harmonious combination of Internet and middleware technologies.

1.4 Object-oriented Modelling (OOM)

In today's industrial world, everyone wants to develop distributed information systems. The appearance of the PC at the start of the 1980s was the element which initiated this movement. The emergence of the Internet in the mid-1990s, the software and marketing element, was the detonator. Everyone can see the advantage of distributing not only data, but also applications. Yet, although there are many advantages, a major disadvantage appears: complexity.

> *Distributed systems are complex to design and manage.*

- Complex in design. A large system (or application) can contain a large number of components. It is necessary to define the functions offered by each one of them by making reuse an objective. It is also necessary to have a global view of the system in order to understand its execution flow.

- Complex in management. The personnel in charge of the production of information systems in a company view the emergence of distributed software with trepidation. Currently an application is monolithic. When it does not function correctly, the system manager knows on which machine to look. Let us imagine the case of an application composed of components that are distributed across a network. In the case of failure of this application, on which machine should one look? How does one know all the components and their location?

In order to reduce this complexity, it is useful to use a *methodology*. The interest in the one presented here is twofold: it supports the design of distributed systems, but also, and this constitutes its originality, it provides the information necessary for the management of a distributed information system during production.

1.4.1 An Object-oriented Method for the Design, Integration and Management of Client–Server Applications

The proposed method is called MethodF[10] and has been defined by Digital Equipment Corporation. As with every software development method, MethodF contains phases for requirements, specification, design and implementation. Its principal characteristics are the following:

- It starts with the requirements of the system to be constructed and continues as far as the generation of code. It also includes the management aspects of the final system (see Fig 1.22).

- It is object oriented. The principal advantage in our eyes of the concept of an object is that it forms a common language between a domain expert, for whom the application is constructed, and the computer person.

- The object model that is obtained is the domain expert's system, with its invariants (objects). This model is totally independent of the way in which it will be implemented.

- The requirements for the system to be constructed are organized according to the concept of scenario introduced by Ivar Jacobson in his Object-Oriented Software Engineering (OOSE) method.

---

[10] MethodF is a registered trademark of Digital Equipment Corporation.

- The notation used in the specification and design phases come from James Rumbaugh's Object Modelling Technique (OMT) method.

- This method is only really useful if it is used in conjunction with a software modelling tool (for example the ObjectPlus tool from Palladium or ROSE from Relational). Such a tool allows:

  o the storage of models constructed during the design phase;

  o the reuse of all or part of already existing models. Thus the concept of reuse is applied, not at the programming level, but at the design level;

  o the automatic generation, during the implementation phase, not only of the code for objects (for example, in C++), but also of the IDL code describing the inter-object communication protocol.

- During the specification phase, the dynamic behaviour of the objects is modelled. This valuable information is used later by the management tool.

The management of distributed applications is a new problem for which we can use, by adding necessary functions, existing tools for system management. This is further eased when the tool is object oriented.

1.5 Conclusions

The aim of this book is to show the importance of middleware as a technology allowing us to answer the current needs of industry. These needs are expressed in terms of distribution and co-operation between applications or between application components.

Different technologies that implement middleware are presented and analysed. It seems that their use profoundly influences the global architecture of an information system. It implies a change of culture since it changes the structure of applications.

The advantages which result have a cost; this cost is complexity. The fact that we can use a complete methodology (Fig 1.22) integrating the problems of design and reuse of software and the management of the system in the production phase must reassure every information system manager who will have, sooner or later, to go down this path. The gains are related to the amount of effort required.

In this book, no reference is made to software performing direct access to data stored in remote databases. These products are supplied by database manufacturers and seem useful because their use is simple. However, they overload the network by transferring a great deal of useless information and they lead to the mixing of the functions of processing and those of data manipulation. Their architectural utility is weak. Moreover, for these products whose purpose is *transfer of data*, no standard exists. The focus of this book is *the unification of processing, not of data*. The chapters which follow this one describe in greater detail the technologies presented in this chapter.

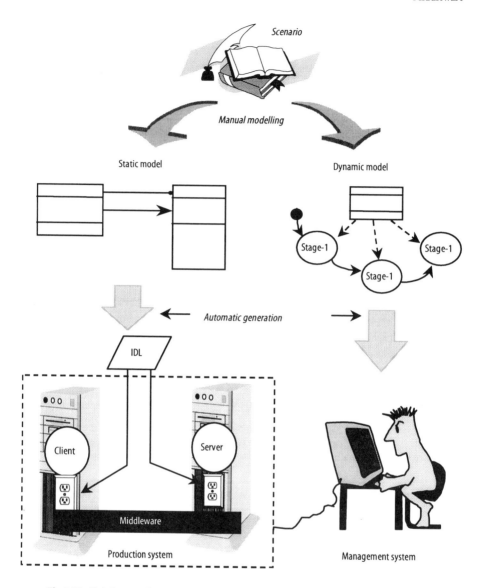

Fig 1.22 Global approach to the design, construction and management of a distributed system.

2. *Message-based Middleware*

Message-based middleware was one of the first technologies to develop the concept of a common communications mechanism allowing applications to exchange data across the network without having to know the basic primitives. No standard has been defined for this technology, and it is only through existing products that its characteristics can be discovered.

These products, which allow the exchange of messages in two possible ways, can be divided into three categories:

1. *Products in which the passage of messages is performed directly from the sending to the receiving programs.*

2. *Products performing message storage in waiting queues. In this approach the receiver is no longer a program but a waiting queue.*

3. *Products implementing the above two methods.*

The model which uses waiting queues is unanimously preferred to the other because messages can be sent without the destination program being available. For this reason, this model is considered in this chapter.

2.1 Introduction

The goal of information processing in a company is the realization of the company's objectives in financial terms. The continual changes which affect the markets in which the company operates have consequences for its internal information processing. They induce the use of new applications which offer functions that were desired. These new pieces of software must be able to exchange information with existing software. The communication structure between applications then takes on a considerable importance because it conditions the ways in which a new piece of software is added.

Currently, many information systems have a point-to-point communications structure (Fig 2.1). In this structure, every communication between two applications A and B implies the existence of a specific connection (L). This connection (L) is characterized by the existence of a communications interface for each of the two applications I_A and I_B and of a mechanism for transferring data (M). The addition of a new application imposes the introduction of communication

31

interfaces into the code of the existing applications that want to communicate with it. This equally implies the creation of new mechanisms for the exchange of data. From this fact, the point-to-point structure appears too inflexible (addition of applications is difficult) and costly in terms of system management because each connection must be individually handled.

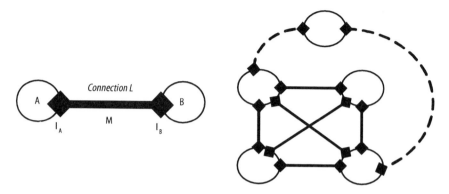

Fig 2.1 Point-to-point communication structure.

2.2 Principal Functions

The solution proposed in waiting-oriented middleware consists of defining a single communications bus to which each application connects via a well-defined attachment point, called an interface. During a dialogue between two applications, each sees the other through its logical communications interface and does not know its physical address.

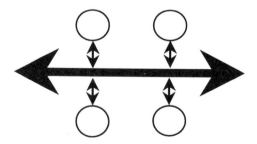

Fig 2.2 Single communications bus.

This communications structure is independent of the operating systems of the machines on which the applications reside, as well as of the nature of the transmission network used. In the OSI model, which defines the different levels of communication between information systems, middleware represents the three highest levels – the session, presentation and application layers. It defines the communications protocol between applications (Fig 2.3).

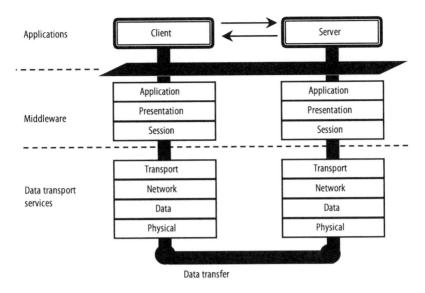

Fig 2.3 Location of middleware within the OSI model.

This inter-application communications structure rests on top of lower-level communication structures such as the network protocols (TCP/IP, DECnet, SNA or OSI) and/or the mechanisms offered by the operating system (e.g., interrupts).

In this organization, applications communicate by exchanging messages. They run independently of each other and independently of the communications bus which, on each machine, takes the form of an executable program. This independence is achieved by use of queues. A queue is an area of memory used to store messages and is managed by the communications bus software. This allows a message to be sent at any time without needing to know if the destination application is available at the moment. The queue works like a mailbox in which the receiving application looks whenever it likes for messages.

2.2.1 Synchronous/Asynchronous Communications

Communication by message exchange can be synchronous or asynchronous. In this model, and from a logical viewpoint, each application is associated with two queues. One allows messages to be sent (output queue), and the other allows message reception (input queue). The dialogue between the two applications goes as follows (Fig 2.4):

1. Application A starts the dialogue. It attaches itself to the two communications queues. This is done using an operation provided by the communications bus or from the middleware (e.g., Attach_Queues). These message queues represent access to the communications bus.

2. The sending application puts the message to be sent into its output queue (e.g, via the Add_message primitive). This message contains, in addition to the data

to be sent, the name of the destination queue. From this moment on, the message belongs to the middleware and the application can either continue with its internal processing (asynchronous communications) or wait for a reply (synchronous communications).

3. The program which operates the application bus reads the message and transfers it across the network to the destination queue.

4. After being connected to its queues, the destination application waits for messages. When a message is available in its input queue, it reads it via a primitive operation (e.g., Read_message).

5. After processing the message that it has received, the receiving application can return a message to the sending application. In this case, it becomes a sender itself and puts a message in its output queue (e.g., using the Add_message operation).

6. The middleware picks up the message that has been handed to it and transmits it to the application that started the dialogue.

7. The application which started the dialogue is either waiting for the reply and reads the return message as soon as it arrives, or is engaged in processing and will come to read the message later (e.g., the Read_message operation).

The communications scheme described in Figure 2.4 assumes that the application A hopes for a reply from application B. This is not necessarily always the case. An application can send a message to another application without waiting for a reply.

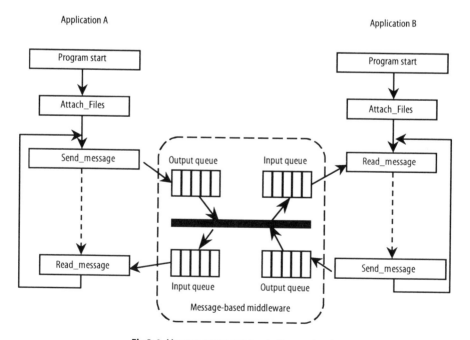

Fig 2.4 Message queue communications protocol.

2.2.2 Message Delivery Guarantee

The combination of an asynchronous communication mechanism and the assurance that a message will be delivered to its destination is at the centre of the current success of message-based middleware. In this communications model, the sender of a message is sure that the message will be delivered to the destination. However, the middleware does not make any guarantees as to when it will be delivered. The time of delivery depends on far too many parameters: load and availability of the network, availability of the middleware and of the receiving application.

The guarantee that no message is lost is obtained by storing them on the disk on both the sending and receiving machines (see Fig 2.5). When the sending application puts a message into the output queue, it is automatically copied to disk. The message is then transferred to the input queue of the receiving application and copied onto a local disk. The message copy on the original disk is then deleted. When the receiving application reads the message in its input queue, it is removed from the local disk.

This mechanism for backing up messages to disk protects against any crash in middleware, of the network of computers and protects against the possibility that the receiving application is not running.

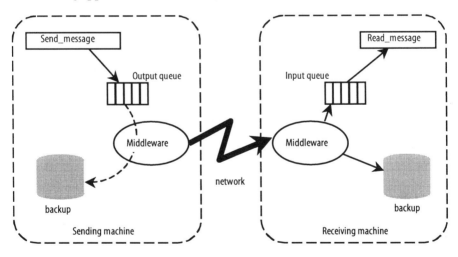

Fig 2.5 Architecture guaranteeing message delivery.

2.2.3 Different Communication Structures

Message-based middleware is based on a logical bus organization allowing different forms of communication. Thus it is possible to:

- Message broadcast. This function of message broadcast lets an application send a message in a single operation to a set of applications connected to the bus. For example, in the middleware product *DECmessageQ*, the list of receiving applications is formed by those applications which, when installed, have been specially registered to receive such messages.

- Share an input queue between several applications. This function allows several identical applications to access the same input queue. This has the purpose of improving the response time of a system by authorizing parallel processing of messages. This approach avoids having to construct a complex application that contains several execution streams (*multi-threaded* application).

- Selective reading of messages. An application is not required to read their input messages in their order of arrival. Selection criteria based on the message origin, its priority, or on a user-defined convention, allows the user to change the order in which messages are read.

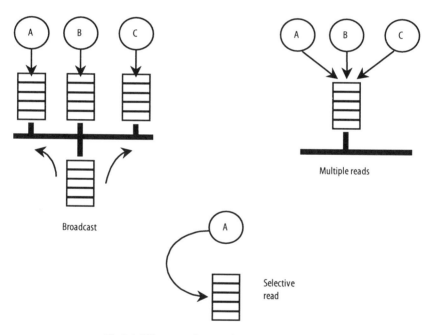

Fig 2.6 Different mechanisms for handling messages.

2.2.4 Structure of a Message

A message is a data structure that is exchanged between applications. The designer of an application defines the content of the message which consists of several parts:

- the data provided by the sending application;

- the attributes characterizing the message and which are used by the receiving application;

- the context added to the message by the communication system and which is transparent to applications.

The exchange of messages permits peer–peer communications; that is, each application can take the initiative in the dialogue. Thus between two applications A and B, at any given time, application A can have the initiative in the dialogue; then at another time, application B can take it. This differs from the master–slave model in which the initiative always stays with the master.

Communication can be synchronous or asynchronous. It is synchronous when the application sending the message waits for a reply message. It is asynchronous when the sending application continues its processing without waiting for a reply.

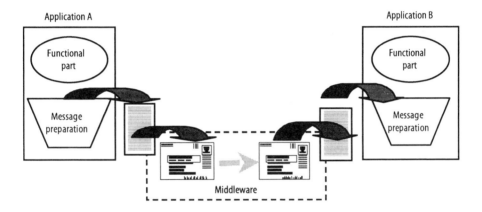

Fig 2.7 Message queue middleware has no knowledge of a message's contents.

Communication using message passing requires that the communicating programs agree on the structure of the messages exchanged between them and on the interpretation of the messages. A fundamental point is that the communication system does not know the content of the messages. The communication system's job is simply to deliver them to the right place. An immediate consequence is that the message must be constructed by the sending program and interpreted by the receiving one. This has the following advantages and disadvantages.

Advantages

- Programs exert tight control over the structure of the messages. In particular, this allows the use of only those functions that are strictly useful in a given context of use. For those who want faster execution, this represents an advantage because it allows the optimization of the dialogue by removing the extra demands placed by a general communications mechanism.

- Messages can be constructed dynamically. The structure of messages does not need to be fixed when the program is compiled.

Disadvantages

- The code in applications mixes the functional part and the part dedicated to communications. This is not correct from a conceptual viewpoint and uselessly increases the amount of work in developing the application. The application's programmer should not have to bother with the details of the communication mechanism. It would be desirable for the communication mechanism to offer more functions in order to simplify the programmers' task. For example: functions for converting data formats are sometimes necessary between communicating applications. Thus for some data that is exchanged (e.g., for character strings), there exist two formats: ASCII and EBCDIC). The exchange of character strings between two systems using two different formats implies that the conversion of one format to another must be taken into account. This conversion activity constitutes a significant part of the process of communication. People who prize the quality of the code and the reduction of the time required for development consider that this work should not be in the hands of the application programmer.

- The application interface summarizes the set of messages which it can handle. It has no formal representation which gives the name of each service and its associated parameters.

2.3   Evaluation of the Principal Products

A very complete document comparing the main message-based middleware products has been compiled by Information Design Inc.[1] We will here only consider those points which seem important in the context of this book. The three products that are evaluated are DECmessageQ from Digital Equipment Corporation, MQSeries from IBM, and TopEnd from NCR.

2.3.1 DECmessageQ

The DECmessageQ product from Digital Equipment Corporation is a software bus using queues. It allows task-to-task communications between processes executing on the following processors: OpenVMS, Digital UNIX, HP-UX, OS/2, AIX, MS-Windows, Windows-NT, Macintosh, Solaris and SunOS.

A common interface allows the exchange of messages either by local communications (inter-process communications), or over the network using the TCP/IP or DECnet protocols.

---

[1] Message Oriented Middleware (MOM) Product Evaluation Report, Information Design Inc., April 1996.

DECmessageQ is the oldest message-based middleware (it was introduced in 1986) and from this fact it is the most stable and the richest in terms of functions offered. Its main characteristics are:

- speed of message transmission;

- synchronous or asynchronous transmission of messages;

- maximum message size of 4 Mb;

- concept of message priority;

- selective reception of messages based on the number of queues and on priority;

- concept of shared files accessible via the MRQ function (Multi-Reader Queues);

- use of a naming system that is local to a machine;

- different options are available for delivery of messages (assured delivery or not);

- queues are organized by group (maximum number of groups is 32,000) and each group can have up to 999 queues;

- use of a clock to manage message delivery time – if the time predicted for the delivery of a message is exceeded, then an alert message is sent to the sender;

- utilities to handle the network and the flow of messages.

In its latest version, the DECmessageQ product will include the following functions:

- Self-describing messages. These messages will contain all the information needed so that the receiver knows how to decode their content. This allows sending and receiving program designers to avoid agreeing on the exact structure of previous messages. Thus, the sending program can add data to a message and change its size without having to re-program the receiving program. This mechanism also allows the handling of changes to data formats between different platforms.

- Global naming system. The possibility of naming queues by name and not by address is extended to all machines. The goal of this is to make it easier to move an application from one machine to another.

- The strong points of DECmessageQ are its availability on all major platforms on the market and its ease of use.

2.3.2 MQSeries

MQSeries is a software product for message-based communication using message-based middleware from IBM. MQSeries is a recent product (introduced at the end of 1994) and is mainly available on IBM platforms. Its principal characteristics are:

- availability on certain platforms, that is: HP-UX, AIX, OS/2, OS/400 and MVS/ESA;

- integration with the CICS transaction monitor;

- automatic starting of processes (this is particularly useful to change the number of servers on demand – when a certain number of messages are waiting in a queue associated with a server, an additional copy of that server is automatically created);

- conversion of data between platforms;

- different options are available for delivery of messages (assured delivery and unassured);

- synchronous or asynchronous message transmission.

MQSeries offers a large palette of functions for the exchange of messages between applications. Its limitations appear principally at the level of its installation and its management which requires both a good knowledge of the platforms and of the product.

2.3.3 TopEnd

TopEnd was designed by NCR which exploited its expertise with transaction handling. This product is written in ANSI C and has the following characteristics:

- Distributed transaction management. TopEnd is the only one of the three products to implement the concept of a transaction between heterogeneous platforms. It uses the DTP (Distributed Transaction Processing) model from X/Open. TopEnd implements the *two-phase commit* which allows the updating of several databases running on different machines.

- Considerable availability. Applications can be automatically duplicated in order to reply to the request. Furthermore, an application which stops can be automatically restarted.

- A high level of security. TopEnd uses Kerberos[2] which is a standard utility for the authentication of users.

- Easy administration of the entire environment thanks to a powerful set of graphical tools.

- Synchronous and asynchronous message transmission.

TopEnd implements transactional communications which differentiates it from the two other products we examined above. This function being very complex, it is not without consequence for the difficulty of installation, use and management of this product.

---

[2] Kerberos was developed by the Massachussetts Institute of Technology (MIT).

2.3.4 Some Comparative Tables

From the fact that no standards exist for this technology, the choice of a message-oriented middleware product is, for the most part, conditioned by the platforms on which it will have to run. Tables 2.1 and 2.2 show the machines, operating systems, and the network protocols on which the three products run. The evaluation in these tables is denoted in the following fashion:

A: Additional functions available   B: Function exists
C: Minimal function exists   –: Function unavailable

Table 2.1 Network protocols used by message-based middleware tools.

Network Protocol	DECmessageQ	TopEnd	MQSeries
TCP/IP	B	B	B
LU6.2	C[1]	B	B
DECnet	B	–	C[3]
X.25	C[2]	B	–

[1] DECmessageQ LU6.2 is available through an extension called LU6.2 Port Server. This product provides an interface between LU6.2 and DECmessageQ.
[2] DECmessageQ X.25 is available via the Q-Adapter product.
[3] Currently available in MQSeries level 1.

Table 2.2 Platforms on which the message-based middleware tools are available.

Platform	DECmessageQ	TopEnd	MQSeries
HP_UX - HP9000	B	B	B
Solaris - SPARC	B	B	–
SunOS - SPARC	B	B	C[2]
Digital UNIX - Alpha	B	–	–
AIX - RS6000	B	B	B
SCO - Intel	C[1]	–	C[2]
OpenVMS - VAX	B	–	C
OpenVMS - Alpha	B	–	–
OS400 - AS400	C[1]	–	B
MVS - System 390	B[3]	B	B
Windows 3.x - Intel	B	B	C[4]
Windows-NT - Intel	B	B	C[4]
Windows-NT - Alpha	B	–	–

[1] Available using Q-Adapter.
[2] Currently available in MQSeries level 1.
[3] Client implementation.
[4] Does not allow use of DLLs.

3. *RPC-based Middleware*

The advantages of distributed processing no longer need to be demonstrated. However, its realization imposes the requirement that we define the unit of distribution. With message-based middleware, this unit is the application itself since this middleware allows communication between applications. During the design of a new application, the problem of defining the unit of distribution occurs. Since programs are decomposed into procedures, they appear as the ideal candidates for distribution.

3.1 The Client–Server Model

The structure of a single communications bus between distributed entities imposes no constraint on who communicates with whom and how. Thus in message-exchange based middleware, any application (A) can take the initiative in a dialogue with any other application (B). Now this must nonetheless be written in the code for applications (A) and (B). Because of this, the question arises as to the definition of a communication bus which automatically takes into account these aspects. Such a bus would have to have the following characteristics:

- the dialogue between two entities is well-defined;

- an entity always has the initiative in the dialogue (master entity) and the other is always waiting for a request (slave entity);

- the slave is organized in such a way as to reply to well-defined requests.

In this communication model, the slave can only satisfy well-defined requests. This aspect is formalized by saying that the slave entity offers services and that they are described in an interface. For this reason the slave entity is called a server. The master is that which requests a service by sending a request. It forms the client. The set forms the client–server model (Fig 3.1).

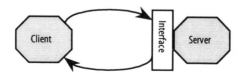

Fig 3.1 The client–server model.

The client–server model works as follows:

- The server publishes via its interface the set of requests that it can satisfy. A service is associated with each request.

- The client sends a request to the server asking for the execution of a service.

- The server executes the service associated with the request and returns the result to the client.

In this model, the dialogue is always initiated by the client and the communications substrate is not defined. It can be assumed that there exists a means for the exchange of messages from the client to the server and vice versa. We note that this client–server model can clearly be implemented using message-based middleware (see previous chapter). The suggestion here is to simplify the code of the communicating entities in order not to have to program this communication structure which is already known at the time the application is designed.

3.2 Client–Server and Procedure Call

The code of a well-structured application can be decomposed into two parts: the main program and the set of the procedures (or sub-programs) which it calls (Fig 3.2). In the traditional processing model, the main program and its procedures are compiled and linked in order to create a single executable entity. During execution, the main program calls the procedures in turn, passing them input parameters. The procedures execute and return their results to the main program in their output parameters.

The concept of remote procedure assumes that the procedures and the main program form two separate executable entities. This means that these two entities belong to two distinct address spaces which do not allow direct exchange of call parameters to procedures. It is therefore necessary to have a communication substrate connecting these two entities and this substrate constitutes remote procedure call middleware.

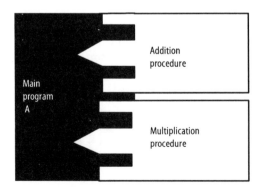

Fig 3.2 The code of an application decomposes into a main program and procedures.

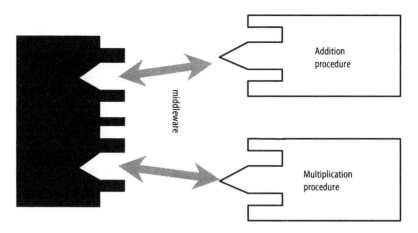

Fig 3.3 The main program and procedures form distinct executables.

A first interesting point to note in this model for distributed processing is that the application code (main program and procedures) remains unchanged, whether the procedures are distributed or not (Fig 3.4). This is the case for the simple reason that the application contains no code related to the communications system.

Remote procedure call implements the client–server model:

- The main program calls services which are the procedures (e.g., Addition and Multiplication). As such, the main program constitutes the client.

- If it is assumed that the procedures are linked to form an executable, then this offers a set of services (e.g., the two services Addition and Multiplication). This executable forms the server.

- The interface of the services offered is completely defined. It is, in fact, the headers of the procedures themselves. This header is also called the service's signature. In our example, the interface of the service contains two signatures which are those of the two services Addition and Multiplication.

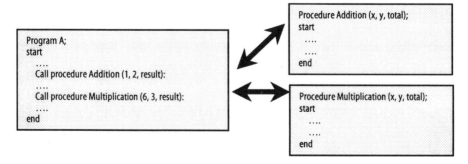

Fig 3.4 Distributed procedures, application code remains the same.

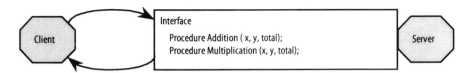

Fig 3.5 Interface in the client–server model.

3.3 Principles of the Remote Procedure Call Architecture

An important characteristic of the implementation of the client–server model in terms of remote procedure calls is that the code of the application remains the same if its procedures are distributed or not. This property is due to the fact that the whole communication system is external to the application code. These are the primary components of this structure which are of interest to us here.

RPC Client

In our example (Fig 3.2), the code of the main program calls two procedures (Addition, Multiplication). In the distributed model, the compilation of the main program is followed by the link phase. At this level, the absence of the two procedures leads to two errors. In order to avoid these errors and to be able to handle all the aspects of communication, two dummy procedures called Addition and Multiplication are added. These procedures are referred to as *client stubs*.

A client stub is a procedure which has the name of the real procedure that it replaces in order to:

- give the impression to the main program that the procedure which it calls is really local;

- replace the code of the real procedure by other code. This new code will handle the connection with the middleware bus in order to send call parameters for the procedure that it replaces to the machine where the procedure actually resides and to collect the parameters returned from the procedure.

RPC Server

The RPC server contains the distributed procedures. In our example, it is composed of two procedures, Addition and Multiplication. However, it is not possible, if the laws of programming are to be respected, to generate an executable program that is composed only of procedures. A main program must exist. Such a program is created and is called the *server stub*. It has a double function:

- allows the creation of an executable containing the procedures which form the server;

- handles communication with the client stub in order to receive the name of the procedure to be called, as well as its call parameters. As a function of the name of the procedure that was received, the server stub activates the designated procedure by passing to it the received parameters. If this procedure returns some values through certain parameters, then the server stub is charged with sending them to the client stub.

The principal components of the RPC communication system are (Fig 3.6):

- The main program of the application. It forms the client. It is the client that starts communication by locally calling a procedure (e.g., Addition or Multiplication). It calls a client stub in fact.

- Client stubs. There exist as many procedures as are called from the main program. The stub is activated by the main program. Its work consists of transferring the name of the procedure that has been called as well as its parameters over the bus.

- The RPC middleware bus which is made up of a run-time system on the client machine and on the server, and of a software network. This bus physically transfers the data from the client to the server.

- The server stub. There exists one and only one per server. It receives data (procedure name and parameters) and locally activates the procedure designated by passing the received parameters to it.

- The remote procedures (in our example, Addition and Multiplication). They are called by the server stub. It is up to them to return the result parameters. They circulate in reverse order to the main program (the client) which receives the results and carries on with its processing.

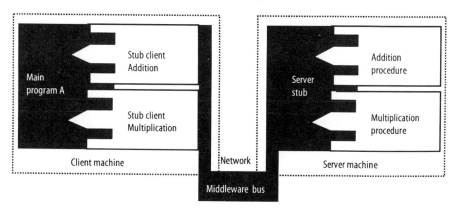

Fig 3.6 Main components of RPC middleware.

3.4 Concept of Contract between Client and Server

The implementation of the client–server model using RPC allows synchronous communications between the client and server. Thus, having called the procedure (service offered by the server), the main program (client) waits for the results. It only continues its execution when the output parameters are returned or when a status message informs it of the termination of the procedure.

The idea of calling remote procedures is very simple and very powerful, but it requires the solution of a certain number of problems before perfect transparency can be offered to client and server. The questions in need of answers are, for example:

- is the procedure call local or remote?
- what is transmitted?
- where is the data sent?
- who receives the data?
- how does one know that the processing is terminated?

In order to reply to these questions and to formalize the dialogue between the client and the server, the concept of a contract needs to be introduced.

3.4.1 The Contract

In the world of commerce, every exchange between client and provider is formalized by a contract. A contract describes the details of the exchange and the obligations of the two parties. Each party signs it and keeps a copy.

In the RPC communication model, a contract is established in order for the client and the server to have the same understanding of the exchanges that they are going to perform. This contract possesses the following characteristics (Fig 3.7):

- It is identified by a unique identification number known as a *uuid* (universal unique identifier).[1] The uuid is used in each request from the client so that the two parties can verify that they are really talking about the same thing (❶).

- It defines and names the interface offered by the server to this client (❷). This interface contains a subset of the services that the server can offer and it contains the signature of the services which the client requires (❸).

- It is written in a special information language called IDL (Interface Definition Language). There exist several versions of this language and one of them was standardized for the RPC technology. It is called OSF (Open Software Foundation) IDL RPC.

- The client and the server each receive a copy of the contract. One forms the client stub, the other the server stub.

---

[1] This number is generated in such a way as to be unique in time and space. It is a combination of the Ethernet address of the machine (which is unique) and the date. This value is associated with the interface. A change in this value indicates that it in fact designates another interface.

- The client and server stubs are sequences of code (most often in C) which have been generated using a compiler for the contract written in the OSF IDL RPC language.

- An interface is a set of procedure signatures whose parameters are characterized by their mode of use (❹): they are either input parameters ([in]), output parameters ([out]), or input-output ([in][out]). Output parameters must be passed by reference (❺) while input parameters are passed by value.

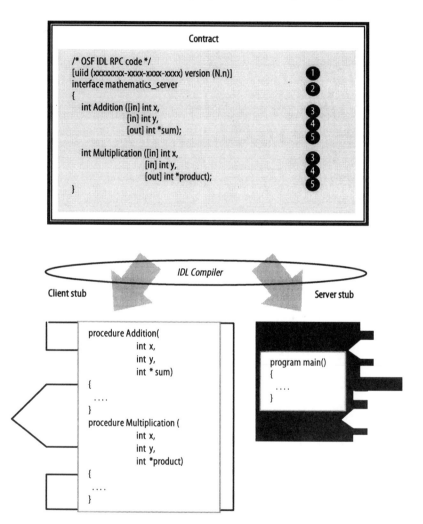

Fig 3.7 The concepts of a contract in RPC middleware.

3.4.2 Construction of Client and Server

The construction of a distributed application using RPC technology requires the programmer to develop three components:

1. The main program for their application (the client). This program can be written *a priori* in any programming language whatsoever. The C language is however the most commonly used because the RPC runtime system is itself written in this language.

2. The set of procedures comprising the application (the server).

3. The contract describing the exchanges between the client and the server. This contract is written in the IDL language.

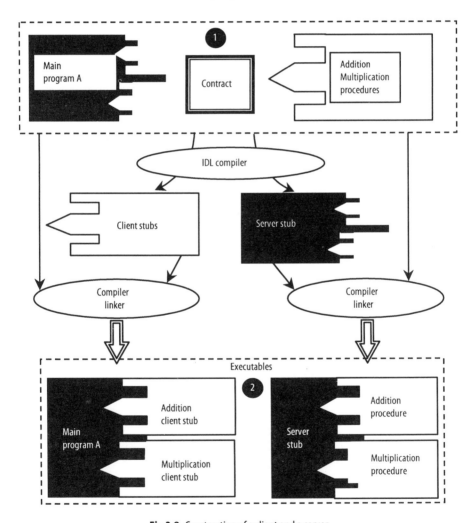

Fig 3.8 Construction of a client and a server.

Figure 3.8 shows how to proceed when the three components mentioned above are available (**❶**). The steps are then the following:

- Step 1: Generate the client and server stubs. This is done with the aid of the IDL compiler.

- Step 2: Construct the client executable. It is necessary to compile the main program and the client stubs and to link the two object code modules thus obtained (**❷**).

- Step 3: Construct the server executable. It is necessary to compile the server stub and the procedures and to link the object code thus obtained (**❷**).

3.5 Structure of Communication

The dialogue between a client and a server makes specific requirements of the client and server. A server represents a specialized entity of relatively large size. On the other hand, the client is not specialized and is usually of small size. This is due to the fact that many clients can exist, while the number of servers is relatively small. If we take the example of a print server for documents; this server is complex and only a few of them need to exist. It has many clients which can be distributed over many machines. On the other hand, a server is generally implemented in the form of a process that is always available, waiting for execution while the client program is activated upon the user's demand.

3.5.1 Data Encoding

An important function of the client stub is to recover the procedure call parameters and to construct the message that will be sent to the server. In this message, all the data is encoded in a standard form.[2] This encoding function has the American name *marshalling*.

This work of encoding is made necessary by the fact that the platform on which the server runs does not necessarily use the same way to represent data as the client platform. To illustrate this, here are some examples of the different ways of encoding data:

- Character data. There exist two standards which are ASCII and EBCDIC.

- The size of words in memory. According to the type of machine, the size of a memory word can be 16, 32 or 64 bits.

- The way in which bytes are numbered in a memory word. Two completely opposed systems exist and are called *big-endian* and *little-endian* (Fig 3.9).

---

[2] Different standards exist. OSF DCE RPC uses NDR (network data representation). Sun RPC uses XDR (external data representation).

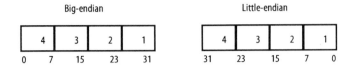

Assumptions:
- Memory words of 32 bits.
- The element with highest value is denoted by 31.

Consequences :
The decimal value of the number 4321 is:

- in big-endian notation: $4 + 3 \times 2^{8} + 2 \times 2^{16} + 1 \times 2^{24}$
- in little-endian notation: $4 \times 2^{24} + 3 \times 2^{16} + 2 \times 2^{8} + 1$

Fig 3.9 The two ways of enumerating the bits in a word in memory.

The OSF DCE RPC standard technology uses the policy of "he who receives decides". Thus, the client encodes its data in its own representation and if the server uses another format, it must call conversion routines. This approach has the advantage of only converting data when it is necessary.

3.5.2 Connection to the Server

There are different possible ways (automatic and otherwise) for a client to connect to the server. The automatic method is the only one that is standardized and it will, for this reason, occupy us here.

The automatic connection method assumes the existence of a name server. Such a server associates a logical name with an entity's physical address. Thus the name server can be used to find the physical address of a server associated with RPC middleware.

The use of a name server operates as follows (Fig 3.10):

• The server registers with the name server in order to declare to the name server its physical address and the interfaces that it offers.

• The name server confirms to the server that it is now known. The server then waits for requests.

• The client makes a request to the name server for the physical address of a server, providing it with the name of the server and the number of the interface.

• The name server returns to the client the physical address of a server which satisfies the search criteria.

• The client can then establish a connection with the server.

Such a method requires that the name server be present on the machines where the client and server are in order that these last two can communicate.

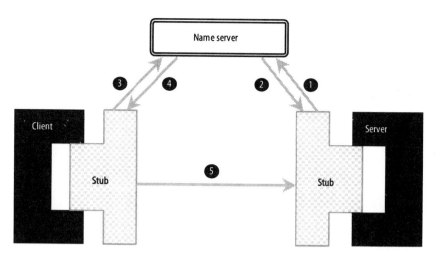

Fig 3.10 Locating the RPC server using the name server.

3.5.3 Synchronous Dialogue

The dialogue between the client and the server is synchronous. When the client makes a request to a server, it assumes that the latter is available, and that it is in a functioning state. This implies that the server is implemented as an already executing process which is ready to satisfy requests. If, however, the server is not in a functioning state, every request from a client will result in an error. Because here, contrary to message-based middleware, no request is saved on disk.

The dialogue between the client and the server is performed as follows (Fig 3.11):

1. The server is activated and its first task is to register with the name server in order to declare its existence as well as declaring the list of the interfaces that it offers.

2. The server starts waiting for requests.

3. The client is activated and sends a request in the form of a remote procedure call.

4. The client stub locates a server offering the desired interface. It obtains the address of the server by contacting the name server.

5. The client stub establishes the connection with the server.

6. The client stub prepares the data, sends it and then starts waiting for the reply.

7. The server stub receives the request.

8. The server stub decodes the data (parameters and the name of the procedure).

9. The server stub calls the procedure by passing its input parameters.

10. If the procedure returns output parameters, they are coded in order to be sent to the client stub. The server returns to the waiting state (step 2).

11. The client stub receives the reply message.

12. The client stub decodes the data that was transmitted.

13. The client stub passes the result parameters to the client's main program.

14. The client continues processing.

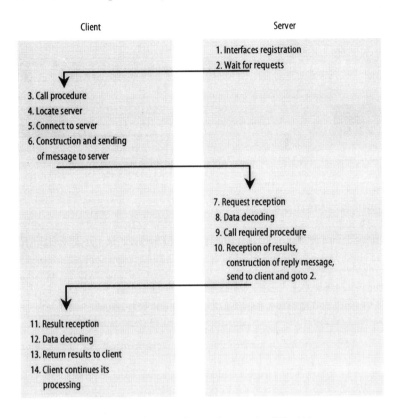

Fig 3.11 Dialogue between client and server using RPC middleware.

3.6 The Standard

The concept of remote procedure has been used by all the major software constructors. In order for their products to be compatible with others, they decided to create a foundation for it and adopted two goals: first, to identify all the functions that are indispensable to the distribution of code and to propose standards for them, and, secondly, to implement these functions and make the code available to the contributing members. This foundation has the name OSF[3] and its choices form standards for distributed technology.

---

[3] OSF is a registered trademark of Open Software Foundation Inc.

The work of the OSF started with the definition of a distributed environment called OSF DCE (Distributed Computing Environment). This environment forms a software layer located between the operating system and the network on the one hand, and the application on the other. From this middle position was born the name of middleware. The DCE layer allows a distributed application to operate as if it were located on a single machine while its components can execute on different machines with different operating systems connected by different networks. The functions offered by the DCE environment are shown in Figure 3.12.

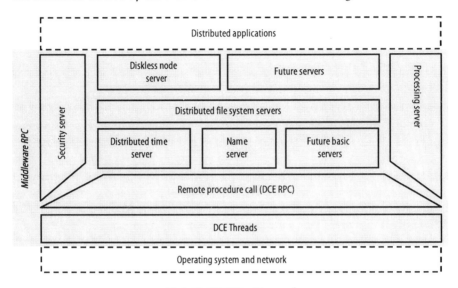

Fig 3.12 OSF DCE architecture.[4]

The services which comprise the DCE environment are modular, possessing a well-defined interface, and are well-integrated. Each service can make a call to the other services in the environment. Thus the RPC mechanism uses the name server in order to declare and locate servers. It also uses the security server to ensure protected transmission of data. It uses, finally, the thread mechanism allowing the execution in parallel of several copies of a single entity.

The order in which the component services of OSF DCE are presented in Figure 3.12 indicates that the services situated in a high layer use services which are situated in a lower layer. Thus DCE threads are used by practically all the other components of DCE.

DCE uses a network service at the level of the transport layer, such as UDP (User Datagram Protocol) or TCP (Transmission Control Protocol). DCE assumes that all the machines in the environment are connected by a reliable network, be it a LAN or a WAN.

---

[4] This figure is taken from Open Software Foundation, *Introduction to OSF DCE*, Prentice-Hall.

In the DCE environment, a node, that is a machine, can be identified in a unique fashion by its network address and a program (client or server) can also be identified in a unique fashion, for example by the number of its TCP/IP port.

3.6.1 Configuration of an OSF DCE Environment

The machines participating in a DCE environment are grouped into cells. A cell represents a network of machines that are administered as a single entity. A cell consists of three types of machine which can be differentiated by the software that they execute. It is important to note that the services offered in DCE are themselves structured along client–server lines. Thus:

- User machine. This machine is not specialized and appears as a client to the DCE services offered by the server machine. It contains at least the DCE RPC and DCE threads mechanisms in order to be able to communicate with other machines. In addition, it contains the client software for the other DCE services (see Fig 3.13).

- Administration machine. This machine contains the software that allows the management of the systems for remote handling of DCE services. This implies that it contains client administration software for all DCE services. Being itself a client, it contains all the software that appears in a user machine (Fig 3.14).

- Server machine. This machine contains the software allowing it to offer DCE services to user machines as well as the administration software servers. It contains, finally, all the client software because it can also appear as a client for DCE services (Fig 3.15).

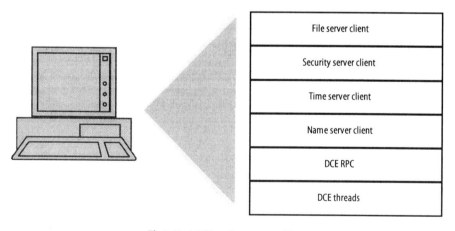

Fig 3.13 A DCE services user machine.

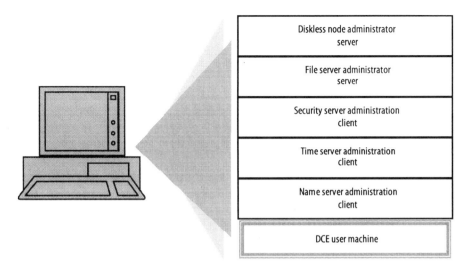

Fig 3.14 Administration machine for a DCE cell.

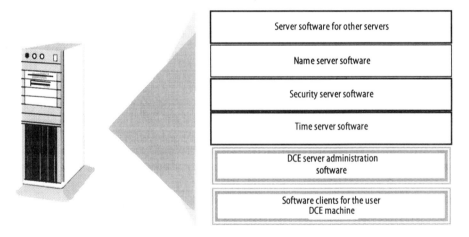

Fig 3.15 Server machine for DCE services.

In a cell, in addition to RPC mechanisms and threads, the following services must necessarily appear: name server, security server and the distributed time server. Figure 3.16 shows a possible cell in which two machines appear. The one contains the distributed time server and the other the name server as well as the security server.

The components of DCE divide into two categories: distributed programming tools (DCE threads and DCE RPC) and distributed services (name server, time server, security server, distributed file server, diskless node server).

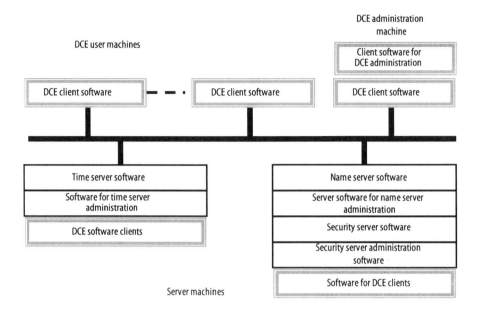

Fig 3.16 Example DCE cell configuration.

3.6.2 DCE Threads

When it executes, every traditional IT application only has a single thread of control. This means that, at any time, there is only a single point in the program which executes. It can be interesting to construct programs allowing the parallel execution of certain parts of the program. Let us take the example in Figure 3.17 in which requests are sent to a server by two clients. To satisfy the request from the first client, it begins its processing. If the request coming from the second client arrives before the end of this processing, this request is left waiting until later. If the server is programmed to offer several control streams (or threads) then a second executable form of this same server is started and can immediately satisfy the second request.

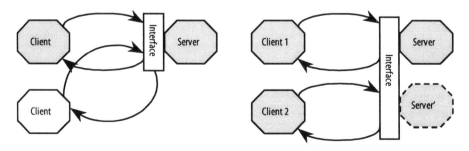

Fig 3.17 Importance of DCE threads.

Let us note that the mechanism offered by DCE threads is applicable to the client as well as to the server. Thus, instead of being blocked waiting for the reply to its request, a client can start another thread and continue with its processing.

Generally, the thread mechanisms are part of operating systems. In this case, DCE uses whatever is available. However, while an operating system does not offer this function which is essential to all other DCE components, it is included in DCE.

3.6.3 Name Server (DCE Directory)

All the resources (e.g., machines, application servers, users) available in a distributed system are listed in a central database associated with the name server. This comprises two main parts:

1. The Cell Directory Server (CDS). This server handles the names of the resources belonging to a cell. It knows, for example, the TCP/IP port number of an application server.

2. The Global Directory Server (GDS). This server allows the enlargement of the name server beyond a cell. A resource in a cell can thus access resources that are external to this cell. This server is based on the international standard CCITT X.500/ISO 9594. It appears as a server operating at a level higher than the CDS server. When a reference to a name is not satisfied at the level of the cell, this reference is transmitted to the GDS server.

DCE operates also with another standard name server called DNS (Domain Name Server) which is much used in the Internet world.

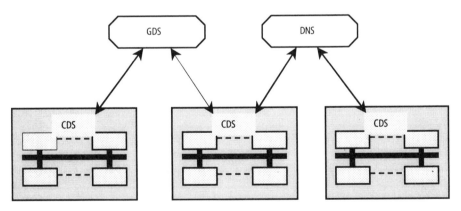

Fig 3.18 Name service in DCE locally uses CDS and globally uses GDS and/or DNS.

3.6.4 DCE RPC

OSF DCE RPC is composed of two types of software: development tools and runtime software. The development tools are composed of an interface definition language called OSF IDL RPC, with which a compiler is associated. The code generated by it forms the stubs which automatically construct the messages to send across the network and which interpret them on reception. The runtime component consists of the network protocols which allow the client and server to communicate. It also contains the software for the automatic generation of names (uuid) identifying an interface in a unique fashion.

3.6.5 Distributed Time Server (DCE DTS)

The concept of time is important in all information systems. It is used, *inter alia*, in order to determine whether an event A occurs before or after event B. On each machine there is a clock which allows a unique temporal reference to be provided. In a distributed environment consisting of several machines, the clocks on each of them must be synchronized for none functions perfectly. The distributed time server in DCE handles this problem in the following way:

- it has a periodic synchronization mechanism for the clocks on the machines belonging to the same cell;

- it allows the maintenance of the idea of time which is as close as possible to exact time. This concept of exact time was standardized and is called *universal time co-ordinated* (UTC).

DCE DTS allows the machines belonging to a single cell to have the same concept of time, and this concept is very close to that of universal time.

3.6.6 Security Server

Security in a distributed environment is complicated by the fact that the messages exchanged across a network can be intercepted and/or modified. The problems pertaining to security fall into three categories. These are the problems of authentication, authorization, and communications security.

- Authentication. The goal of this service is to establish, for two inter-communicating entities, the truth of the identity of the other. Thus, when a client A communicates with server B, the authentication server is able to:

    o assure client A that the server which calls itself B is really server B;

    o assure server B that the client which pretends to be A is really client A. Note that this service uses Kerberos, which is an authentication service implemented at MIT as part of project Athena.

- Authorization. When the identity of an entity (e.g., entity A) has been recognized, it is necessary to verify that it is properly authorized to use a given resource (e.g., resources managed by server B). This verification is performed by the privilege or authorization service. On the other hand, a list controlling access is associated with each resource. This list contains the name of the entities that are authorized to access them. This approach allows, for example, a user of a file to give authorization to another user to access the same file.

- Security of transmission. Security of transmission of data over the network is obtained by integrating with the RPC mechanism encryption mechanisms and mechanisms for detecting access violations. There also exists a login utility which allows the establishment of a secure environment for the user.

3.6.7 Distributed File System (DCE DFS)

The distributed file system forms a client-server application which uses basic DCE services (RPC, name service, security service). The goal of this service is to offer users access, shared or not, to files stored on a file server, located somewhere on the network. The name of a file is unique in the system. The fact that the environment is distributed allows the increase in reliability by duplicating files on several machines. It also allows a user who is limited in disk space to store their data on other machines.

DCE DFS includes a physical file system called the LFS (local file system), which allows one to:

- store the modifications performed on a file during its processing in order to reconstruct it when there has been a system, application or machine crash;

- duplicate files with the goal of improving the reliability of the system or to reduce the access time for users;

- ease the management by the system of files by grouping the files into small entities which comprise the *fileset* and the *aggregate* (a fileset is composed of files and store areas whose total size must not exceed the capacity of a disk. An aggregate is the unit of storage on a disk. It can contain several filesets);

- associate the access control lists at the level of a file or of a disk. These lists add an additional level of security to the system.

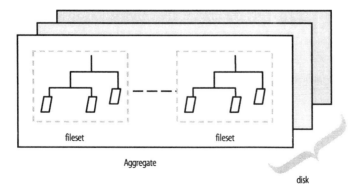

Fig 3.19 Structure of a distributed file system in OSF DCE.

3.6.8 Diskless Node Service

The diskless node server allows such a machine to operate by using the disks on another machine. In order to replace the local disks, it is necessary to be able to offer several other functions. It is necessary, first of all, to allow the machine to start, that is, to load the operating system from a remote disk. Next, it is necessary to obtain the configuration data for the system. It also consists of having access to the distributed file system and finally to allow swapping, that is, the possibility to temporarily store programs on disk.

4. CORBA: Standard Object-based Middleware

The third paradigm for the distribution of systems is based on the concept of object which, here, represents an encapsulation of processing functions. Middleware supporting remote execution of operations on objects is called ORB[1] (Object Request Broker). The standard for this technology is called CORBA[2] (Common Object Request Broker Architecture).

This chapter assumes that the reader has a minimal knowledge of object technology. If this is not the case, the reader is invited to read Chapter 9, Introduction to Object Technology, before proceeding with this chapter.

4.1 Introduction

CORBA describes an architecture and gives the specifications for processing objects distributed over a network. CORBA is also an international standard for which several companies offer software products. Digital Equipment Corporation can be cited, as can Hewlett-Packard, IBM, BEA Inc. and IONA Technologies as well as SunSoft. Other companies offer products which provide all or part of the functionality described in CORBA.

CORBA belongs to a new generation of software which allows *plug-and-play*; that is, the ability to easily connect software modules together. This goal is achieved by combining two technologies: object technology and distributed processing. The result constitutes distributed object processing which inherits the advantages of the two sub-ordinate technologies.

Chapter 9 illustrates the object-based approach which is characterized by a powerful modelling methodology (see Chapter 10), by encapsulation and by inheritance mechanisms.

Distributed processing has, in its own right, long used remote procedure call (RPC) mechanisms (see Chapter 3). CORBA introduces a new paradigm for distribution in which the distributed entity is not a procedure or a set of procedures but

---

[1] ORB is a registered trademark of the Object Management Group.
[2] CORBA is a trademark of the Object Management Group.

an object. This very powerful paradigm has raised many problems for which CORBA offers a solution.

CORBA implements the client–server model by introducing an intermediate entity called a *broker*. The request sent by the client is received by the broker which transmits it to the server. The presence of this broker allows the isolation of clients from servers. Thus, every application (client) can inter-operate with another application (server) without having to know either its address or the way in which the latter performs its task (see Fig 4.1).

Fig 4.1 Client–server model with an agent.

In this model, the client sends a message to the broker asking for the execution of a service. In object language, this is translated into a request to execute an operation on an object. The role of the broker is to identify a server capable of offering such a service and to transmit the request to it. In this model, the client does not know the address of the server (and vice versa). Only the broker needs to know their respective addresses. Thus the client and the server can be running on the same or on two different machines that are connected by a local or a wide-area network.

4.1.1 CORBA and Distributed Processing

CORBA adds to the possibilities for distributed processing in many ways. In particular:

- Clients and servers do not have to know of each other. This allows the addition of new clients and new servers to an existing system without having to modify any of those services already present. Only the intermediary broker must know the address and the functionality of each one. From this fact, this information does not have to be stored in client or server code.

- It allows synchronous and asynchronous communication. The choice of communication style between a client–server pair is left to the developers. In general, the disguising of existing applications in the form of objects leads to the use of asynchronous communications.

- The concept of client–server is highly dynamic. Thus, the same piece of code can appear as a client in one exchange, then as a server in another.

4.1.2 Origin of CORBA

In April 1989, the Object Management Group (OMG[3]) was created in the form of a non profit-making association. The objective of this association is to define and promote standards for object orientation in order to integrate applications based on existing technologies.

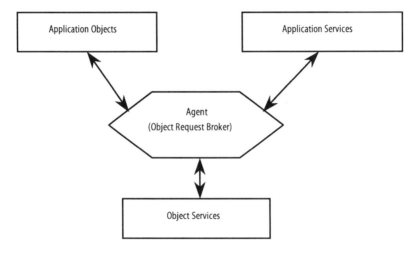

Fig 4.2 The four elements of the Object Management Architecture.

In November 1990, OMG published the *Object Management Architecture Guide*. This document defined an object-oriented architecture called the Object Management Architecture (OMA) (see Fig 4.2) which can be characterized by four separate elements:

- The object request broker (ORB). This broker forms the controlling element of the architecture because it supports the portability of objects and their interoperability in a network of heterogeneous systems. This was the first element in OMA to be implemented as a software product.

- Object services. These are in fact specific system services for the manipulation of objects. For example, they allow the creation of objects and the control of access to them, or, equally, the manipulation of their addresses. Their goal is to simplify the process of constructing applications.

   The members of OMG have published a document specifying an initial list of object services. This document is called *Common Object Services Specification*

---

[3] OMG is a registered trademark of the Object Management Group.

Volume 1 (COSS 1). The following services are defined in it: object naming, object events, life cycle of an object, persistence of objects. A second list was subsequently published, containing extensions to the functions that are offered (see section 4.5, *Object services*).

- Application services. These services offer a set of facilities for allowing applications access to databases, to printing services, or to synchronize with other applications.

- Application objects. These objects allow the more rapid development of applications. A new application can be formed from objects in a combined library of application services to which are added objects belonging to the application itself. Only the latter must be constructed. The application objects are built by software vendors and are not provided by OMG.

The broker specification (ORB) in the OMA model was published in 1991 in a document called *The Common Object Request Broker: Architecture and Specification, Version 1.1*. This document was written in a collaboration between Digital Equipment Corporation, Hewlett-Packard, Hyperdesk Corporation, NCR Corporation, Object Design Inc., and SunSoft, and reviewed by other members who now number around 700.

Version 2.0 of this document was published at the end of 1994 in order to clarify certain points, in particular communications and inter-operability between brokers when the latter come from different manufacturers (see section 4.4).

4.2   The CORBA Conceptual Model

CORBA separates the client process from the server process so that one can be modified without affecting the other. CORBA separates the way something is requested to be done from the way in which the task is performed. Thus, a CORBA client only knows how to ask for something to be done and a CORBA server only knows how to perform the requested task. This allows one to change the way in which a server performs a task without altering the way in which a client actually asks for it.

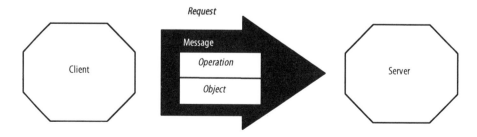

Fig 4.3 Communication between client and server.

The separation between client and server is guaranteed by the fact that these two entities communicate by means of requests. A request is a message sent by the client to the server. This message contains the name of an operation and the name of the object on which the operation is to be applied. In CORBA every interaction is based on the sending of requests (see Fig 4.3).

4.2.1 The Concept of Interface

Requests sent by a client and to which a server responds are described in what is called an *interface*. An interface represents a contract between a client and a server. This contract defines the operations on objects that the client can ask for and that the server undertakes to perform. Thus, in CORBA, the interface is object oriented because it describes the operations which can be performed on a certain type of object. This interface is written in a particular language called the Interface Definition Language (IDL).[4]

An interface describes a system object. An object system appears, therefore, as a set of objects isolating the client from the server. In particular, clients are isolated from parts of code which represent the services (or operations on objects).

```
Interface Employee
{
void promote (
        in char new_post
        );
void demote (
        in DemotionCode reason,
        in string description
        );
};
```

Fig 4.4 Example of an IDL interface.

An interface can have attributes. The purpose of an interface is to define the actions that are possible over an object, so two access operations are automatically associated with each attribute: an operation to read its value, and one to write to it (when the attribute is not declared *read_only*). Figure 4.4 provides an example of an interface constructed in the IDL language. This interface defines two operations associated with the object *Employee*, namely *promote* and *dismiss*.

Since the interface represents a contract between a client and a server, each must receive a copy of it in order to be able to justify their actions. In the example shown in Figure 4.5, this means that:

- the client possesses a copy of the *Employee* interface and can make a request in order to *promote* or *dismiss* an instance of the object of type *Employee*.

---

[4] This language is also called OMG IDL. It should be noted that it is different from the RPC IDL language.

- the server offering the *Employee* interface knows how to execute the operations *promote* and *dismiss* on all instances of type *Employee*.

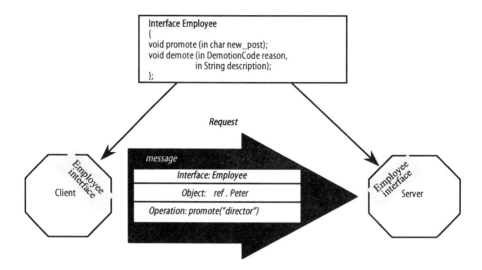

Fig 4.5 Example of a client request for an instruction to promote Peter.

Let us recall that an instance of an object is an implementation at execution-time of an element of a given class. Thus, Peter and Paul can be two instances of class *Employee*. In CORBA, object instances are identified by a reference. If, for example, a client asks for the promotion of the Peter instance, in its request it must specify the reference to Peter, the name of the interface to be used and the name of the operation to perform, together with its parameters (Fig 4.5).

4.2.2 Structure of a Server

In the CORBA model, a server is an entity which allows the satisfaction of requests. These requests are expressed in an object language in the form of a request to execute an operation on an object. The piece of code implementing an operation is called a method (see Chapter 9). A server is, therefore, composed of methods and one of them is activated when an operation on an object is requested.

In order to fully comprehend the mechanism used in CORBA, let us consider the example of a client containing the reference to an instance of type *Employee* called Peter (Fig 4.6). This client possesses a copy of the contract which describes the *Employee* interface. From this fact, it knows that there exists a server offering the two operations *promote* and *dismiss* for every instance of type *Employee*.

Otherwise, there exists a server implementing the *Employee* interface. This server knows how to execute the methods corresponding to the two operations belonging to this interface. It can therefore satisfy every request requiring the execution of one or other of these operations on every instance of type *Employee*.

In this context, the client application can, for example, send a request requiring the promotion of the instance Peter. This request is received by the broker (ORB) which locates the server implementing the *Employee* interface, and which sends the request to it. The server has two methods associated with the two operations described in the *Employee* interface. It must be noted that nothing prevents a server from offering several methods for the same operation. CORBA defines the mechanisms for selecting the method to be used for any given request. The method *PromoteEmployee* is executed (this means, for example, that the status of employee Peter is changed in the database) and a message confirming execution is returned to the broker which sent it to the client.

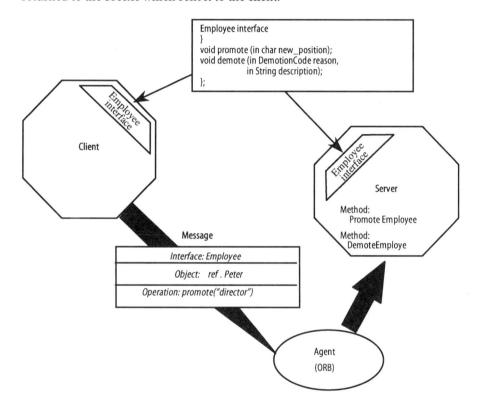

Fig 4.6 Example of a client–server dialogue in CORBA.

4.2.3 Definitions of the Principal CORBA Components

Let us review the principal components described in the CORBA model.

Client (or Application Client). This is any entity capable of generating requests asking for the execution of operations on some objects. A client contains one or more interface definitions, each detailing which operations are possible on which objects.

Interface. It describes which operations are possible on which types of object. Interfaces are described in the object-oriented Interface Definition Language. Thus, the mechanisms of inheritance also apply to interfaces.

Reference to an object. This is, in fact, a reference to an instance of an object. In distributed systems such as CORBA, it is desirable to pass the reference to an object rather than the object proper in order to optimize the amount of data that needs to be transferred. A reference contains the information necessary to specify an object in a given ORB. Thus, two ORBs (brokers) coming from two different vendors can have a different representation for object references.

Broker (ORB). It acts as an intermediary between the client who sends a request for the execution of an operation and the server which executes the method associated with this operation. This broker can itself be centralized or distributed.

Request. This is a message sent by the client and directed by the broker to the appropriate server.

Object system. This is a system of objects isolating clients from servers by means of a well-defined interface.

4.3   The CORBA Architecture

Figure 4.7 shows a request sent by a client and whose destination is a server.

The server contains the code and data that form the implementation of the object. The broker (ORB) is responsible for all the mechanisms which allow the location of the server, of preparing it to receive the request, and for the transfer of data to the server. The client, knowing the *Employee* interface, knows that it can send a request to an instance (e.g., of Peter) to which it holds the reference, asking for the execution of an operation (e.g., promotion). This request can be generated in two ways: statically or dynamically.

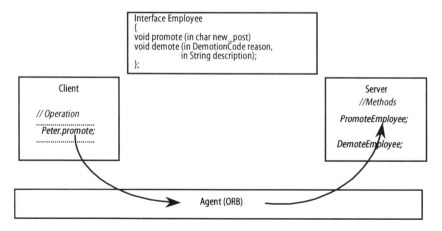

Fig 4.7 Example of a request sent by the client and transmitted to the server by the agent.

4.3.1 Static Invocation

Static invocation is very similar to the RPC mechanism (see Chapter 3) because it allows synchronous and *one-way* communication (one-way communication is a message to which there is no associated response) and it assumes the existence of stubs at the client and server levels (Fig 4.8). The client stub makes the connection between the client and the agent. The server stub (called the skeleton in CORBA terminology) makes the connection between the agent and the server. Thus, the request from the client passes through its stub in order to arrive at the agent. The agent sends the request to the server via its skeleton.

Static invocation assumes that communication between client and server is pre-defined; that is, known when they are constructed. The client code is linked to its stub in order to obtain a single executable module. Symmetrically, the executable module of the server is the result of linking the code for the methods with that for the skeleton. It turns out that if a server receives requests in static mode from n different clients, this server must possess n skeletons. All the same, if a client wants to communicate with p distinct servers, it must possess p stubs.

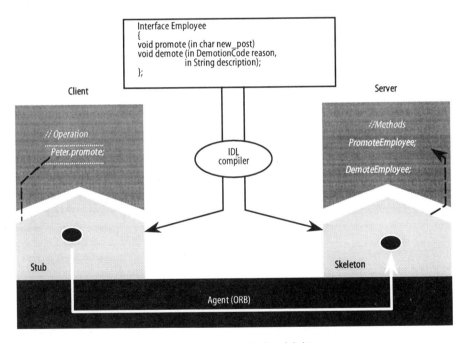

Fig 4.8 Static invocation. Stub and skeleton.

4.3.2 Dynamic Invocation

The client can also invoke the server in a dynamic fashion. This approach is very similar to the mechanism used in message-based middleware (see Chapter 2). In this type of invocation, the client has no stub connecting it to the server and must dynamically construct its request. To do this, the client uses the broker's dynamic invocation interface. This interface provides access to a database containing the description of the interfaces of all the servers that are available in the system. The client thus finds the description of the operations that are possible on objects. The construction of the request is in its hands. It comes about that the client code contains a piece of code solely dedicated to the construction of requests.

The database containing the interfaces is loaded from descriptions of these interfaces in the IDL. Its main goal is to allow, at runtime, a client to determine the existence of interfaces that were not present when it was constructed. This allows the addition of new servers which can be used by existing clients, without modification to their code, provided they are programmed to use dynamic invocation.

In dynamic invocation, the client has no stub, but, on the other hand, the server must have a skeleton. This latter is generated in the same way as in static invocation.

Static and dynamic invocation use the same semantics at the request level. From this fact, the server cannot distinguish the invocation mode. During dynamic invocation, the agent verifies that the request is correctly formulated/stated.

Dynamic invocation allows three styles of communication: synchronous, asynchronous (also called deferred synchronous), and one-way.

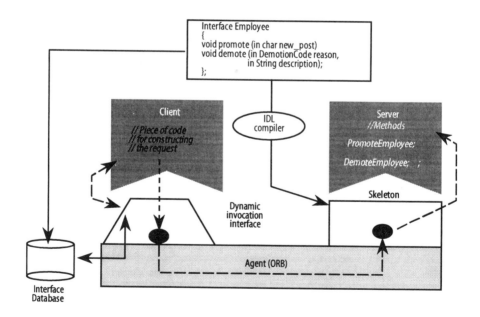

Fig 4.9 Dynamic invocation. Existence of an interface database.

4.3.3 Server and Object Adapters

The server provides all the components of an object, that is, the code for the methods and, for each instance, its data (attributes). In the model proposed by CORBA, methods can be implemented in different ways: by a program, by wrapping up an existing application, by a library, by an object-oriented database, etc.

The server also contains procedures to activate or deactivate objects. It must also be able, for example, to create new object instances, make them permanent or manage their access. To help it in its task, CORBA provides a set of services by means of object adapter intermediaries (cf. Fig 4.10).

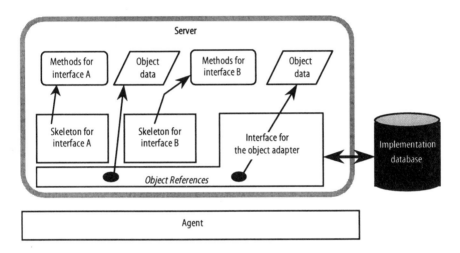

Fig 4.10 Structure of an object adapter and associated service.

The object adapter must offer all the services which the server needs. The level of service offered depends on the software product used to implement the agent. If a given service belongs to the agent, then the adapter will offer an interface for its use. Otherwise, the adapter must itself contain this service. Specialized adapters can be developed in order to take advantage of the basic services offered by ORB. The main ones are:

- Basic object adapter. It offers the set of services necessary for conventional servers. It allows the association of a program with each method as well as permanent memory for each instance.

- Object adapter for libraries. This allows access to files and therefore does not offer activation and identification services for objects.

- Object-oriented database adapter. It is linked to a database in order to access the objects stored there.

It results that in the same environment, several object adapters can coexist.

Object adapters have an interface described in the IDL and must provide the following functions:

- Starting and stopping servers. The information describing the composition of servers is stored in the implementation database. This is updated when installing servers. When a request comes to an adapter, the latter activates the targetted server if it is not already active.

- Verification of client identity. The adapter knows how to identify the client by its request and verify that it really has the right to execute the operation that it has requested.

- Generation and interpretation of object references. A given ORB uses its own representation of a reference and this must be converted into the programming language used to write the method on the server operating on the referenced object. To do this, the adapter uses information located in the implementation database.

- Invocation of methods. The correspondence between the operation requested by the client and the method to be executed as well as the selection criteria are described in the implementation database. A parameter passed to this method indicates the selected instance which allows the location of data belonging to this instance. The other parameters that are passed depend on the definition of the skeleton. When the execution of the method terminates, return parameters or an error message are returned to the client.

Thus, there appears a new entity called the implementation database. This database is updated during the installation of a server and is used to satisfy requests. Figure 4.11 shows everything necessary to incorporate clients and servers.

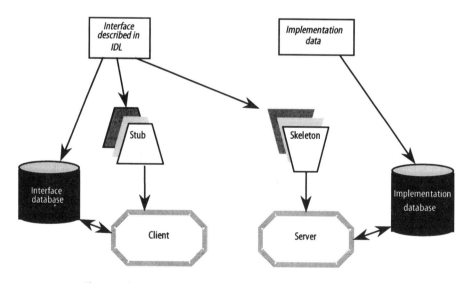

Fig 4.11 Elements necessary to the implementation of a client and a server.

4.3.4 General Structure of the Agent's Interfaces in CORBA

The client and the server in the CORBA model inter-operate with ORB via a set of standard and non-standard interfaces. They are:

- Interfaces that are identical in all ORBs. Dynamic invocation and the ORB interface. The ORB interface allows direct communication between the client, the server and the agent. This interface provides access to functions common to clients and servers. These functions mainly deal with references to objects which are opaque to the client and server (they do not understand the structure of a reference). Moreover, a reference to an object can be structured in different ways according to the software used to implement the broker. All this leads to offering functions allowing the conversion of these references into a format that can be used by clients and servers.

- Interfaces depending on the agent. All the connections with the agent's central component are dependent upon its implementation. It will be observed that clients and servers do not directly communicate with this central element. This point is central because it has the consequence that every application composed of a set of clients and servers running with a particular implementation of the CORBA software will run without modification on a CORBA from another vendor.

- Stubs and skeletons. For any given type of object, there exists a skeleton and one or more stubs. Their interface depends on the description of the object in the IDL.

- Object adapters. There can exist several object adapters and they, by construction, are not standard. Only the basic object adapter is standard.

Figure 4.12 shows the different interfaces associated with the agent in CORBA.

4.4 The CORBA 2.0 Standard

In the CORBA model, the client talks to the local broker (on the same machine as the client). This broker must determine on which machine is to be found the server and then communicate with the broker local to that machine. It is the latter which communicates with the server (Fig 4.13). In this mode, the broker (ORB) is distributed: it has a representative on every machine in the system.

The first CORBA standards (1.0, 1.1 and 1.2) were mainly interested in the client–broker and server–broker interfaces. The broker appeared there as a black box whose implementation is left to the judgment of the designers and sellers of software. This approach has the merit that it allows the portability of applications between different CORBA products. This means that an application composed of client and server objects, running on the CORBA middleware from company X, can correctly operate without modification with the CORBA middleware product from company Y.

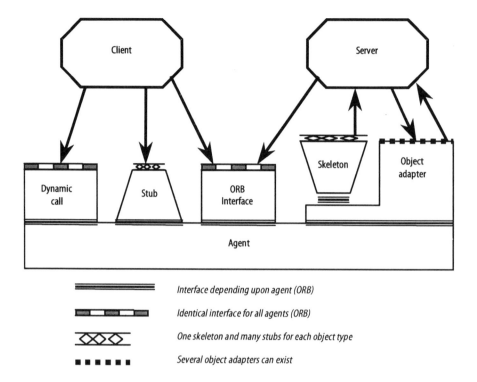

Fig 4.12 Interfaces of an agent (ORB).

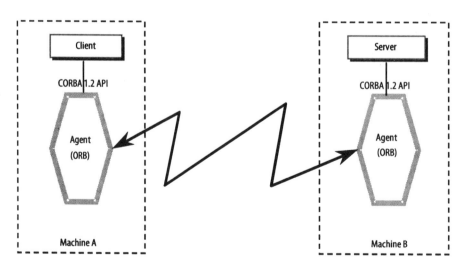

Fig 4.13 Distribution of CORBA agents.

However, these standards do not specify how an agent which is distributed, that is, having representatives on several machines, engages in dialogues of an internal nature. It is, consequently, impossible to combine middleware products from different vendors. The brokers in middleware X have their own mode of communication and are incapable of communicating with brokers in a middleware product Y from another vendor. The goal of CORBA 2.0 is to improve upon this state of affairs.

On 6 December 1994, there was a vote at OMG with the effect of recommending a technology allowing the inter-operability of brokers as part of the project of defining the CORBA 2.0 standard. The chosen technology was the GIOP/IIOP protocol[5] in the case where TCP/IP is used as a transport protocol. As an option, a protocol based on DCE RPC is also recommended – the DCE-CIOP.[6] The choice is thus biased in favour of a newly defined protocol – one which has not yet been implement or tested, and offers no services such as network management or naming – rather than on a protocol which is already widely distributed, rich in services and recommended by numerous users. It is important to observe that OMG has chosen a minimalist operation which does not exclude other transport protocols. It is only on TCP/IP that it has been possible to find an agreement (Fig 4.14).

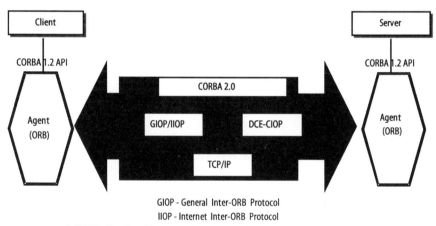

Fig 4.14 CORBA 2.0. Protocols for inter-agent inter-operation.

It is to be noted that existing products use different protocols. Thus the DOE (Distributed Object Environment) software from Sun uses ONC RPC on top of TCP/IP. The ORBPlus product from Hewlett-Packard uses DCE RPC. DSOM (Distributed System Object Management) from IBM uses TCP/IP directly, NetBIOS or IPX/SPX. The ObjectBroker product from Digital is based on TCP/IP.

---

[5] General Inter ORB Protocol/Internet Inter-Orb Protocol.
[6] Distributed Computing Environment – Common Inter-ORB Protocol. This protocol is a subset of the functions offered by the DCE RPC technology.

Let us note finally that other object models exist, the most important of them being the Component Object Model (COM – see Chapter 5) from Microsoft. This model uses DCE RPC as its transport protocol. The choice of the same protocol for CORBA by OMG would have greatly facilitated the inter-operability between objects in the CORBA and COM models.

The CORBA 2.0 standard does not only include inter-operability between brokers. It specifies the interface for agents, the interface for dynamic invocation, the interface for the two databases (interface and implementation), object adapters and the connection between the programming languages (currently C, C++ and Smalltalk).

4.5 Object Services

An agent (ORB) allows the direction of requests from clients to servers. However, the communication between client and servers requires another level of services. These additional services are implemented in the form of objects connected to the broker, and are described by an IDL interface. Thus, there arises a concept of an extended software bus, combining broker and service objects, capable of offering a rich set of communications functions to connected application objects.

OMG has considered a certain number of services which form the object services part of OMA (Fig 4.2). Some were standardized (naming, persistence, life cycle, event notification) at the start of 1994. Others have since been standardized (security, transaction, multiple access, relational). Here is a brief description of each of them:

- Object naming. This service establishes the correspondence between the logical name of an object and its internal reference. This service was conceived on the basis of pre-existing services (DCE CDS, ISO X.500 and Sun NIS+).

- Persistence. This service ensures the persistence of an object beyond the existence of the process which created it. The state of an object is protected in permanent memory (disk) and restored upon demand.

- Life cycle. This service offers all the functions required to handle an object: creation, destruction, moving, copying, etc.

- Transaction. This service is indispensable for implementing highly reliable business applications. It allows one to be assured of the consistency and integrity of a transaction between objects (the ACID[7] properties). Up to now, these functions are offered by transaction monitors for entities which are not objects.

- Event notification. This service allows objects to register as waiting for certain events. Thus when an event occurs, the objects having signalled their interest

---

[7] ACID stands for *A*tomicity, *C*onsistency, *I*solation, *D*urability.

in it, are loaded. An event is generated by an object and is directed to other objects which are not necessarily known to it.

- Security. This service allows control of access to an object by identification of the client and by handling of a list defining the authorized clients.

- Multiple access. This service allows the handling of parallel access to one or more objects.

- Relational. This service allows the expression and handling of associations between objects (for example, relations between a container object and the objects it contains).

- Management of object licences. Since objects are created by software products, their use must be managed.

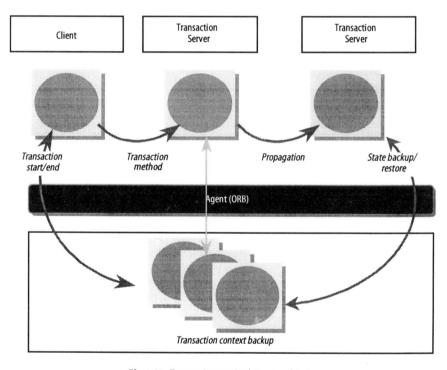

Fig 4.15 Transaction service between objects.

5. OLE/COM: Object-based Middleware from Microsoft

OLE/COM is the object-based middleware from Microsoft. It is based on the object model called COM (Component Object Model). As this model is fundamental, this chapter is mostly about it.

5.1 Introduction

The acronym COM has two meanings. For Microsoft, it means the *Component Object Model* which forms the object model underpinning the OLE[1] version 2.0 middleware. Following the agreement between Digital Equipment Corporation and Microsoft concerning the definition of a common object model, the mark COM also denotes the *Common Object Model*. The latter is in fact an extension of the object model present in OLE 2.0. Thus the two definitions associated with the mark COM only denote the same model at different stages of its evolution.

The first version of OLE (called OLE1) was designed to allow composite documents (for example, documents containing text and images at the same time) to be handled. The second version of OLE (OLE2) was intended simply to improve on the functions offered by OLE1. OLE2 introduced a highly generic object model whose use can be extended well beyond the handling of composite documents. Thus, OLE2 offers a set of interfaces (object-oriented) which allow applications to inter-communicate. The first implementation of OLE2 required applications to run on the same machine. However, nothing in the underlying object model prevents applications from being distributed on different machines. This observation led to an implementation of a distributed OLE2 middleware running at the same time on not only the Windows-NT platform, but also on UNIX.[2]

The study of OLE/COM object-based middleware requires us to concern ourselves with the COM object model which forms the infrastructure on which rest the OLE component technologies.

---

[1] OLE stands for Object Linking and Embedding. It is a registered trademark of Microsoft.
[2] Microsoft announced a distributed OLE2 for Windows-NT for the second half of 1996. Realizing the importance of object-based middleware, Microsoft financed the development of a version of OLE2 running on UNIX and IBM (MVS and OS/400) platforms. This work was done by SoftwareAG and Digital Equipment (for DEC/UNIX and OpenVMS).

5.2   The COM Object Model

The COM model defines mechanisms for the creation of objects as well as for communication between clients and objects that are distributed across a computer network (it will be observed that COM implements the client–server model in which the client is not necessarily an object – the same as in CORBA). These mechanisms are independent of the programming languages used to implement objects. COM defines an inter-operability standard at the binary level in order to make it independent of operating system and machine.

5.2.1 Interface and Object

5.2.1.1   Concept of an Interface

The concept of an interface defines a set of functions associated with an object. The word interface means the *signature* of these functions, that is, their name and the set of their parameters. An implementation of the interface is formed from the code for these functions. Finally, an *interface instance* is a table of pointers (Fig 5.1). In object terminology, these functions are called "operations" when referring to the interface and "methods" when speaking of the implementation or of code.

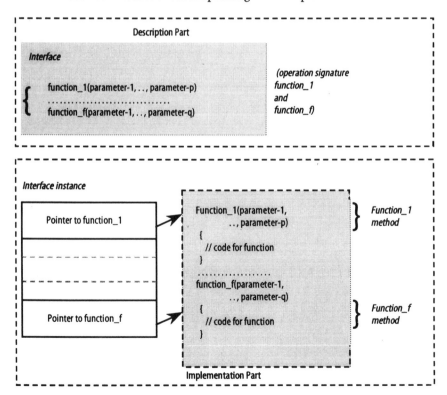

Fig 5.1 Interface, implementation of an interface and instance of an interface.

We can observe that each interface is unique in the system. A Globally Unique Identifier (GUID)[3] allows them to be uniquely named.

5.2.1.2 Concept of an Object

The structure of a COM object can be inferred from the concept of an interface. A COM object has one or more interfaces which a client accesses via pointers. It is not possible to directly access an object itself. The body of an object contains the method code as well as the data which belong to it.

A simple object, such as a data object, has a single interface which describes two operations, for example *GetData* to obtain the value of an attribute and *SetData* to write its value (note that there is no standard function defined in COM to access object attributes). A more complex object, such as a composite document object, has at least three interfaces.

Thus, a COM object is completely defined by the set of interfaces which comprise it. These interfaces offer all the functions which a user of this object needs in order to work with it. A COM object is accessible only through its interfaces.

Figure 5.2 shows the complete structure of an object. In order not to have to re-draw the pointer table forming the instance of an interface each time, a simpler graphical representation is used.[4]

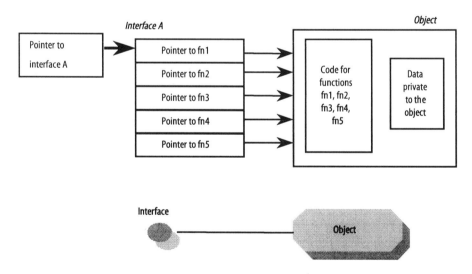

Fig 5.2 Structure and representation of a COM object.

---

[3] This is a 128 bit integer which guarantees uniqueness in space and time for an interface, an object and a class.
[4] This graphical representation of a COM object is used in all the books about OLE; for example, K. Brockschmidt's *Inside OLE2*, Microsoft Press.

In the COM model, clients access objects through the intermediary of well-defined contracts which are implemented by the interfaces offered by the object. To identify the interfaces, COM uses only GUIDs. When an object offers an interface, this means that it knows how to execute all the functions belonging to it and that it provides a pointer to this function to the COM system.

It appears that an interface contractually represents the services offered by an object. It is necessary, however, to observe that:

- *An interface is not a class.* An interface is not a class in the strict sense of the term because a class must allow the generation of object instances. An interface does not allow the direct handling of an instance of an interface. Any class of COM objects must offer an interface and an instance of this class must be generated for the interface to exist. On the other hand, each object can implement a function in its own way as long as it conforms to the definition of its interface (for example, the *Istack* function can be implemented either as a table or as a linked list).

- *An interface is not an object.* An interface is composed of a group of functions which form a standard at the binary level through which clients and objects communicate. An object can be written in any language provided that it provides a pointer to the functions belonging to the interface.

- *An interface has a well-defined type.* Each interface possesses a GUID which uniquely identifies it.

- *An interface is not modifiable.* If a new function is added or if the semantics of an existing function are modified, a new interface is created. So, a new GUID is assigned to it. Hence, there cannot exist several versions of the same interface. We observe that an object can offer several interfaces and can, thus, only have a single method for two functions belonging to two different interfaces. This allows the implementation of progressive revisions to an interface.

- *An interface represents an indivisible, contractual unit.* When an object offers an interface, it must offer all the functions contained in this interface. If an object belongs to a specific class of object (for example, Windows objects or composite objects), it must then include several interfaces which are characteristic for this class.

5.2.2 Access to an Object's Interfaces

When a user of an object obtains a pointer to that object, the pointer only references an interface belonging to the object. The client never obtains a pointer to the object proper. The pointer which is obtained allows access to the functions that appear in the referenced interface. This pointer does not allow access to the data held in the object. Finally, this pointer does not give direct access to the other interfaces of the object. Thus, access to the attributes of an object can only be made via the intermediary of the functions belonging to an interface and each interface must allow access to the other interfaces of the object. To do this, there exists a standard function called *QueryFunction*. This function allows one, given the name of an interface, to obtain a pointer to this interface.

Syntax: *QueryInterface(InterfaceName, &PointerInterface)*
InterfaceName: name of the interface being sought (input parameter);
PointerInterface: pointer to the interface being sought (output parameter)

Let us assume that an object has two interfaces A and B (Fig 5.3). A pointer to interface A is given to a client. This client can only access the functions appearing in interface A (e.g., *QueryInterface* and *fn_1*). In order to access the functions in interface B (e.g, *fn_q*), the client must:

1. know that interface B exists and know its name;

2. request, *with* help from the *QueryInterface* function, a pointer to interface B.

In order for this to be possible, the function *QueryInterface* must appear in every interface.

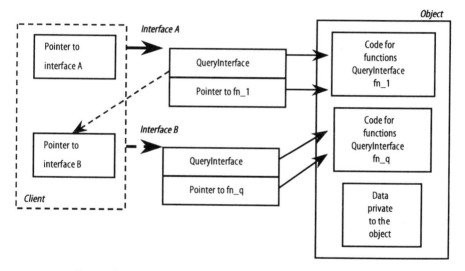

Fig 5.3 The *QueryInterface* function allows access to all interfaces of an object.

The *QueryInterface* function is fundamental to the COM model and as such belongs to the *IUnknown* interface, which is common to all COM objects (for Microsoft, all objects with the *IUnknown* interface are also known as "Windows Objects"). This interface contains all the fundamental functions that every COM object must offer. In addition to the *QueryInterface* function, this interface is composed of two functions, *AddRef* and *Release*, which also appear in every other object interface (they are the first three) (see Fig 5.4). These two functions enable the posting of the clients of an object. Thus:

- *AddRef* increments the reference counter in the object. It returns the number of clients accessing this object.

- *Release* decrements the reference counter in the object and returns the resulting value. It can destroy the object when the value of the counter reaches 0.

- *QueryInterface* returns a pointer to the required interface of the required object (or NULL if the interface does not exist). This function calls *AddRef* to post this new client.

The functions belonging to the *IUnknown* interface must have a complete knowledge of the object because they must be capable of accessing all its interfaces and storing the number of clients currently accessing it.

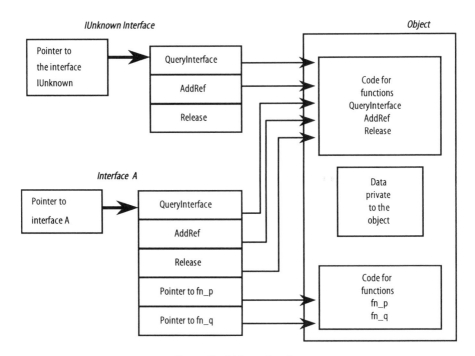

Fig 5.4 The *IUnknown* interface.

The *QueryInterface* function allows the interfaces offered by an object to be known when it is executed. The number of interfaces that are offered by an object is not limited. This allows different levels of communication between objects.

In some cases, the *IUknown* interface is implemented in a way that is independent of the other interfaces. This convention means then that this interface is shown above the object and separate from the other interfaces (Fig 5.5).

At this point, it is useful to recall that an important characteristic of COM is its capacity to continually offer more services. This is possible thanks to the *QueryInterface* function. It allows, thus, a client to ask an object the following question: "Do you offer an interface like this?"

A client can be programmed in such a way that it can make use of all the object functions that it needs for the objects that it manipulates. These objects can develop in stages, without consequence as far as the client code is concerned. An old object will reply in the negative to the second question: "Do you offer an interface like this?" while a new object will reply in the positive. This approach allows the update of objects (for example, by adding new interfaces to them) with no implication at the client code level. The same client, without recompilation, can profit from the newly available interfaces.

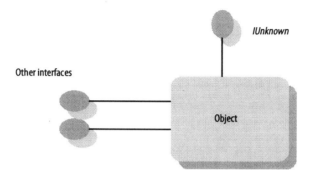

Fig 5.5 Representation of an object with the *IUnknown* interface.

5.2.3 The Infrastructure of COM

The binary level standard is the key to the COM architecture and is what makes it extensible. This standard defines how clients and objects interact. All of this implies that COM also specifies:

- the mechanisms for obtaining the interface using the *QueryInterface* function;

- counting the clients accessing an object by means of the *AddRef* and *Release* functions;

- the rules for memory management. When client and object exchange data across two memory spaces, it is necessary temporarily to allocate buffers in memory.

COM implies the existence of code at the machine's operating system level. This code forms the COM middleware which is organized as a library (implemented in Microsoft Windows using Dynamic Link Libraries (DLLs)) and which consists of:

- A reduced number of basic functions that can be used by clients and servers. The set of these functions forms the API (Application Programming Interface) of the COM infrastructure. For clients, these functions authorize requests for the creation of objects. For servers, they offer the possibility of making newly created objects accessible.

- The server location service. This service allows the determination on the basis of a class identifier, of the name and the location of the server which handles this class. This service has the name *Service Control Manager* (SCM).

- Remote procedure call when client and object are operating in two distinct memory spaces (see section 5.2.5). The RPC technology used is the standard DCE RPC.

- A mechanism for allocating memory for applications. This mechanism allows, in particular, the permanent saving of an object state, which can be restored at any time.

- A mechanism for managing names and for naming new objects. This name allows clients to access an object in the system no matter where and no matter when. The concept of an object *moniker* forms the access bridge for objects. A moniker knows how to establish the correspondence between a logical name of an object and its physical location.

- A uniform transfer mechanism for data. This mechanism is implemented using an interface through which clients and objects can exchange data. This interface also allows a client to ask for an object to send it a message (or event) when an accessible data item is modified.

Thus, the COM middleware allows the creation, storage and the naming of objects. It also allows communication between objects and the exchange of data. Figure 5.6 shows that the components of COM interact between themselves, one function being able to call others.

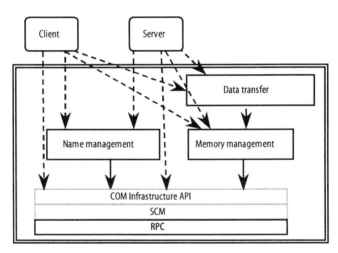

Fig 5.6 COM middleware

5.2.4 First Access of an Object

We have seen, in previous sections, the structure of an object, and how, given an interface, other of its interfaces can be accessed. The question which it is now necessary to answer is the following: "Knowing the existence of an object offering certain functions, how can one obtain a pointer to one of its interfaces?"

In order to answer this question, it is necessary to make the interpretation of the client–server concept in the COM model more precise.

Client: a client is any sequence of code (for example, an application) calling the services of an object. A client can also make requests for services offered by COM in order to ask for the creation of object instances.

Server: a server is a sequence of code associated with a given class of object, identified by a unique *class identifier*. A server knows how to create instances of objects of this class and knows how to associate them with an interface pointer.

In this scheme, a client never communicates with a server. It communicates either with an object in order to ask for the execution of a function, or with the COM infrastructure for the execution of requests. For example (Fig 5.7), a client can send a request to the COM infrastructure asking for the creation of objects of a certain class (❶). COM is able to load into memory and to activate the code of the server associated with this class and transfer the request from the client to it (❷). The server creates an instance of the object (❸) and passes a pointer to one of its interfaces to COM (❹) which it transmits to the client (❺). The client can then access the object interface that was newly created (❻). Thus, client and server never communicate directly.

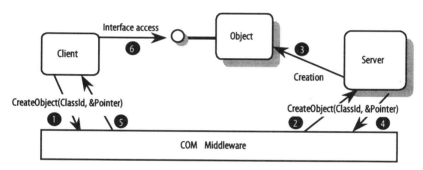

Fig 5.7 Communication structure between client, object, server and COM.

5.2.5 Different Types of Server

There exist numerous differences between a C++ object and one in COM. For example, C++ objects live in a single address space while COM objects can live in disjointed ones. This leads us to consider three types of server for which the object creation and object interface access are identical from the viewpoint of the client, but different at the implementation level.

Client and Server Share the Same Address Space

In this model, the client makes a request to COM to ask for the creation of an object. COM then loads the code for the server into the address space of the client (in the Windows environment, this is possible thanks to the existence of DLLs) and activates the server. The latter creates the requested object locally and returns a pointer which is a local address for use by the client (Fig 5.8).

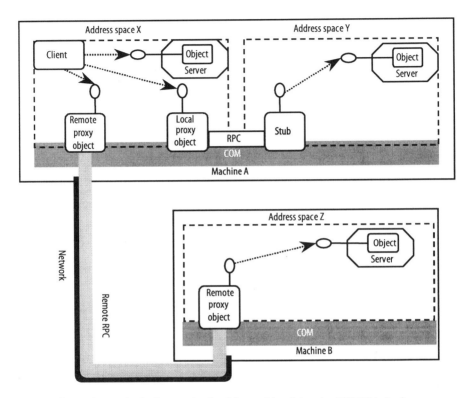

Fig 5.8 Communication between local and distant objects is based on DCE RPC technology.

Client and Server Operate on the Same Machine, in Two Disjoint Address Spaces

In this model, the server constitutes a completely independent entity having an address space that is disjoint from that of the client. A client being able to access only the objects belonging to its own space, the system operates as follows (Fig 5.8):

- The client makes a request to COM to ask for the creation of an object.

- COM realizes that the server is an external process. It locates it and transmits the request to it. The server creates the object in its own address space and returns to COM a pointer to an interface of the object created.

- COM creates an object local to the server called a *stub*. COM gives this object the pointer to the newly created object's interface.

- COM generates an object called a *proxy*, which is local to the client. Such an object is characterized by the fact that it offers the same interfaces as the created object but contains neither methods nor data. Its goal is to receive calls and to transmit them to the stub. Communication between the proxy object and the stub object is performed using RPC technology.

- COM returns a pointer to an interface of the proxy object to the client.

Thus, when the client asks for the execution of a function on a created object, this request is made on the proxy object. This object transmits, using the RPC mechanism, the request to the stub which transfers it to the real object. The latter executes it and the result goes back to the client by following this path backwards.

It should be noted that in this model, the client–object pair exists at the same time in the address space of the client and in the address space of the server. For the client, all this happens as if the target object were local (Fig 5.8).

Client and Server Operate on Two Different Machines

The mechanisms for object creation and for communication between client and objects are identical to those in the previous model. The only difference lies in the fact that communication between the proxy object and the stub is achieved with the help of a remote procedure call (Fig 5.8).

5.2.6 Implementation of Objects

An important characteristic of every object model is its capacity for the reuse of existing objects in order to construct a new one that offers additional functionality. The mechanisms of inheritance form one way of achieving this end. Experience has, however, shown the difficulty of managing complex systems using these mechanisms. COM introduces another approach based on the principle of the black box. In this approach, an object reuses another object without knowing its internal structure. It is only interested in its behaviour.

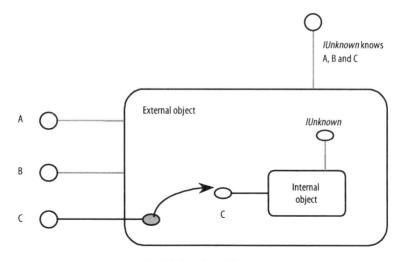

Fig 5.9 Container object.

COM offers two mechanisms which allow the reuse of objects. They are:

1. *Container* object. In this model, an object contains another object. The external object, called the *container*, uses the services of the internal object in order to implement some of the functions in its interfaces. To do this, it is not necessary for the two objects to possess the same interfaces. In fact, the container object uses the interfaces of the internal object in order to implement some of its own interfaces. It can be said, then, that the external object delegates its interface to the internal object. In Figure 5.9, the external object offers three interfaces, A, B and C. The client of this object does not have to worry about its internal structure. Thus the interface C, which is delegated to the internal object, can be known completely using the *IUnknown* interface of the external object.

2. Aggregation. In this model, the external object reveals the interfaces of the internal one as if they were its own interfaces. This approach is useful when the external object delegates each call to one of its interfaces to the same interface of the internal object. In this model (Fig 5.10), the three functions – *QueryInterface*, *AddRef* and *Release* – on interfaces A, B and C of the external object must have the same behaviour as those belonging to the *IUnknown* interface. Thus the *QueryInterface* function from the *IUnknown* interface must know the interfaces A, B and C. This must be the same for the *QueryInterface* function that belongs to interface C. However, this interface belongs to the internal object and only knows the interfaces of this object. In order to rectify this anomaly, when the external object is constructed, the pointers to interface C are modified to point to the external object.

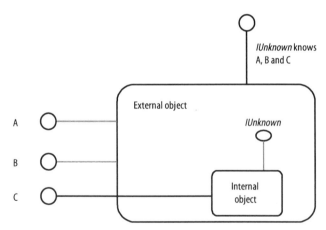

Fig 5.10 Reuse of an object by aggregation.

5.3   OLE2

The development of the Microsoft Windows system towards an operating system that is completely object oriented finds its genesis in the appearance of OLE2. So, a

large number of system functions (e.g., functions associated with the file management system) appear in OLE2 in the form of operations associated with objects.
Currently, these objects are implemented on top of Windows functions; that is,
they form an additional software layer between applications and the system
proper. This has a negative impact upon the performance of applications and is
currently compensated for by development facilities offered to programmers. The
number of system functions that are directly available is very small, the other
functions only appear when a particular object is manipulated. The impact on
performance will disappear when the operating system is completely written as
objects.

OLE2 is organized in layers, each layer exploiting the functions offered by the layer
below. Figure 5.11 depicts the general structure of OLE2. The lowest layer of the
OLE2 model is formed by the COM infrastructure which was described previously
in this chapter. The other components are now to be briefly outlined.

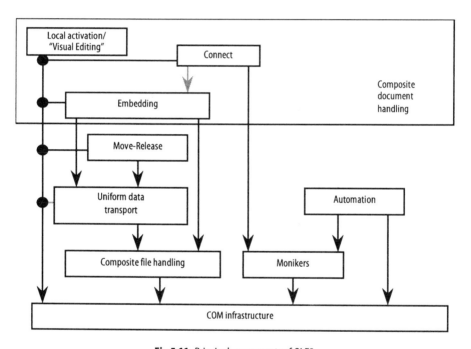

Fig 5.11 Principal components of OLE2.

5.3.1 Composite File Management System

The file management system in OLE2 is made up of a set of seven objects. What
makes it unusual is the fact that a file can, itself, have a hierarchical structure.
Thus, a file can contain other files and/or directories. Files containing data (which
can be of any kind: text, graphics, binaries, etc.) are called *streams*. This hierarchical structure (originally called a composite file) enables documents to be easily

organized. It also enables objects manipulating this document to navigate through its structure.

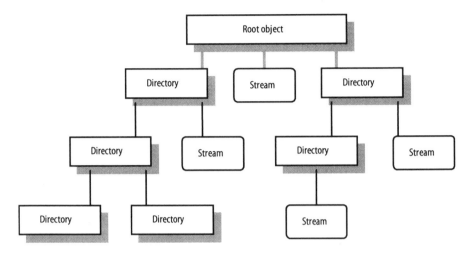

Fig 5.12 Internal structure of a composite file.

5.3.2 Uniform Transfer of Data

In order to regularize the different data exchange mechanisms, such as the clipboard, cut-and-paste or Dynamic Data Exchange (DDE), OLE2 introduces the concept of a data object. These objects possess an interface called *IDataObject* which collect all the existing operations for clipboards, cut-and-paste and DDE. These objects can use composite files as well as main memory to hold the data to be exchanged. The choice of medium used is left to the transmitting entity. Thus, this data transfer technology forms a layer that is constructed on top of the COM infrastructure and the file management system.

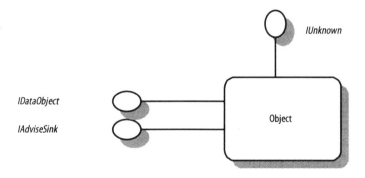

Fig 5.13 Structure of a data object.

This new technology allows the description of the data format, the type of the destination (when it acts as a peripheral) and the transport medium being used. OLE2 separates the work of preparing the exchange from its execution. Thus, new functions allow the transfer of a pointer to the data object from the sender to the destination. Next, data transfer proper takes place.

The destination (or user) of a data object can wish to be informed of every modification performed on this object by the sender. In this scheme, the user does not have a direct connection with the source of the data. They only want to be informed of every change which is reported to them. To this end, OLE2 introduces an interface called *IAdviseSink* which allows the data object to receive notification when some data is modified by the sender. Two types of notification exist: "warm" notifies a modification only; "hot" also includes the data that has been modified.

5.3.3 Management of Composite Objects

OLE2 is formed from a set of elements which define standards. The technology of composite objects standardizes communication between applications on condition that they adhere to the standards described by the lower layers; the COM infrastructure defines inter-object communication; composite files define a standard for the structure of files. Finally, uniform transfer of data standardizes the exchange of information between components.

A composite document represents a collection of different data, with different origins. The technology which allows the manipulation of these documents implements parts "L" (Linking) and "E" (Embedding) in OLE2. A composite document belongs to a *container* application which handles the integration of different data. Each type of data (called document object) is created and updated by its associated application object (e.g., a drawing forms a type of data which was created and which can be updated using PowerPoint[5]).

Document objects can be read or inserted into composite documents. Document objects which are inserted can be locally activated. For example, a report created with MS-Word[6] can contain a drawing created with the PowerPoint tool. This drawing was either incorporated into the text by cut-and-paste and cannot be modified, or was inserted and can then be directly modified in MS-Word which knows how to call PowerPoint.

5.3.4 Automation

The automation technology allows an object to expose its interfaces in such a way that they can be used by other applications. Given an object, it is possible, for example, to know of all of its interfaces as well as their contents, and identify each

---

[5] PowerPoint is a Microsoft software product allowing the construction of drawings and texts for use in presentations.
[6] A Microsoft word-processing application.

operation as well as its parameters. The goal of this technology is to make programming under OLE2 easier. It supports the construction of sophisticated programming tools.

5.3.5 Conclusion

The Microsoft OLE technology was introduced in order to ease the handling of documents. Version 2 of this product has improved inter-operability between applications by extending software components. These software modules, which can come from different vendors, can thus be assembled in order to create new applications. OLE2 represents the first step towards distributed object technology at Microsoft.

6. *Comparison between CORBA and OLE/COM*

Two standards exist in the object-based middleware domain: the official standard, called CORBA, and the de facto standard OLE/COM from Microsoft. Some work is underway to make them compatible. The distributed version of OLE/COM is called DCOM (Distributed Component Object Model). This is the name which will be used in this chapter.

6.1 Introduction

Distributed object models seem to be key elements in the construction of client–server applications. Two major standards[1] are currently available:

- CORBA, defined by OMG (a group which is composed of more than 700 members) for which many products exist, for example: ObjectBroker from Digital Equipment; Distributed System Object Model (DSOM) from IBM; Distributed Objects Everywhere (DOE) from Sun; Distributed Object Management Facility (DOMF) from Hewlett-Packard; and Orbix from Iona Technology.

- DCOM (Distributed Component Object Model) from Microsoft, a *de facto* standard.

CORBA and DCOM allow a client to access distributed objects which do not reside in its address space. Distributed and local objects are handled by them in the same way. Two points are emphasized by them:

1. how a client identifies and accesses objects;

2. how these objects are located.

The fact that the objects reside in different address spaces introduces an additional level of complexity. It must then allow:

- the location of the object – before activating the object's method, it is necessary to locate the object itself;

---

[1] For completeness, we should also mention the Portable Distributed Objects (PDO) from NeXT.

- activation of the method associated with the object – it can turn out to be necessary to load the object code into memory when it is not resident there when the request arrives;

- establish the connection with the object;

- convert the data into a standard format;

- send the message containing the request.

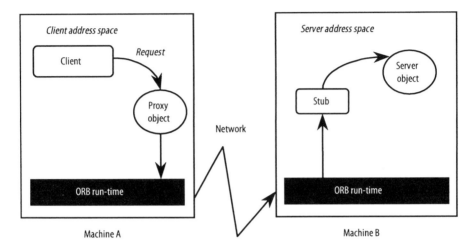

Fig 6.1 Elements common to the CORBA and DCOM models.

Locally (that is, in the same address space as the client), procedure call is enough to implement all the functions described above because some of them become irrelevant. On a single system (that is, on the same machine), a request can be implemented by means of a shared memory communication. For distinct systems, the implementation of a request implies that:

- the network node on which the object is situated must be found;

- a connection with the machine that forms the node must be established;

- data is transmitted over the network.

In this scheme, the destination system can be of a different type from the sender. This difference can be expressed, for example, in the way in which numbers are encoded in memory or in the format used to represent floating point numbers. All of this imposes a data format change called *marshalling*.

In order to implement the mechanisms described above, CORBA and DCOM use the same structure which is based on the concept of *interface* and *proxy* object (see Fig 6.1).When a client wants to access an object belonging to another address space, the concept of a proxy object is introduced. This proxy object is local to the client and is a clone of the target object: it offers the same interface. Its function is to receive requests from the client and to transfer them to the server object. Thus, as far the client is concerned, everything happens as if the target object were local to it. In the address space of the server object, there exists, in a symmetric fashion, a clone of the client (which is called a *stub* in DCOM and a *skeleton* in CORBA). This client clone receives requests transmitted by the proxy object and sends them to the server object.

6.2   Code Reuse: Inheritance and Aggregation

Code reuse is one of the advantages of object technology. Reuse is performed using interfaces describing the operations provided by an object. When an object reuses an existing interface, it reuses, thus, the code associated with the operations belonging to this interface. The goal is therefore to encourage the reuse of interfaces and to do this, CORBA and DCOM allow an object to offer several interfaces. The difference between these two models lies in the mechanisms used to generate these multiple interfaces. CORBA uses the mechanism of inheritance while DCOM uses aggregation.

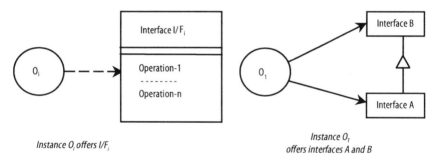

Fig 6.2 Interface inheritance mechanism is CORBA.

6.2.1 Inheritance in CORBA

Let us consider an instance of a class offering a certain interface. This instance offers, by construction, operations belonging to the interface associated with it (Fig 6.2). Let us assume that class A inherits from class B. Every instance of class A is capable of offering the operations associated with class A but is also capable of offering those associated with class B. Thus, in Figure 6.2, instance O_1 offers operations defined in the two interfaces A and B. In this scheme, class B is often referred to as the *root class*.

CORBA, like every traditional object language, uses inheritance as a technique for reusing code. The most general operations are associated with the highest class (root class) in order to be usable by other classes using simple inheritance. It needs to be noted that CORBA also allows multiple inheritance. For example, in Figure 6.3, instance O_1 is associated with class A, and it offers an interface which contains the set of operations contained in the three interfaces A, B and C.

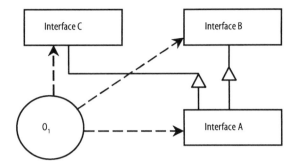

Fig 6.3 Multiple inheritance in CORBA.

Importance of the Root Class

The root class is considered by some (particularly at Microsoft) as the Achilles heel of the CORBA model. Every alteration to this class is automatically introduced into its sub-classes. This assumes very strong control at the level of the root class. Really, the tendency is to encourage the purchase of previously coded classes, and the user becomes dependent on the development of these root classes. Every new version of a root class can contain changes which are not strictly compatible with the previous versions, and these can lead to unexpected behaviours in the instances which use these new interfaces. This is the reason why Microsoft chose aggregation as the reuse mechanism for its software.

6.2.2 Aggregation in DCOM

In the DCOM model, each interface is independent of the others. This leads to a great number of interfaces, each being of a smaller size. This means that an object generally has several interfaces. Any change in an interface affects only the objects which use it, and there is no other induced effect. The effects of any alteration are better managed.

In DCOM, code reuse is implemented using aggregation. An object can contain other objects and offer their interfaces as if they belonged to it. Such an object represents the aggregation of the interfaces of the objects it contains.

DCOM and CORBA offer two different techniques for the reuse of code. The differences between these two techniques are not as clear-cut as might appear at first sight. Thus, an aggregate object can easily use routines from externally developed libraries in its code. Every change to these libraries can affect the objects which use them. On the other hand, a well-designed class must allow compatibility with previous versions. This weakens further the criticisms of the inheritance mechanisms for root classes.

6.3 Composite Document Handling: OLE2 (COM) and OpenDoc (CORBA)

A composite document is a document containing different sorts of data stored in the same file. The management of component documents automatically allows users to make use of applications which are able to manipulate (create, edit) each type of data. This is implemented by inserting each group of data into a document and maintaining links to the applications which supported their creation. This structure allows at any time the modification of the data held in a document.

In a single document, text can coexist with numeric tables produced by a table generator, and with pictures created by a graphical tool. The creator of such a document can, for example, work with MS-Word to edit the text, and then, by clicking twice on a numeric table contained in their document, bring up Excel to modify the table. The vision of the user is concentrated on the document and not on the tools allowing its construction.

The handling of composite documents implements object technology and contains protocols which allow the application handling a document (for example, a text editor) to communicate with applications which allow the creation of the data contained in this document. These protocols must allow applications to share resources such as files or windows on the screen. The structure of a file becomes, therefore, more complex and, as far as Microsoft is concerned, takes the appearance of a container. It is a system of files within files.

The handling of composite documents is of extremely high importance to companies and OMG has decided to work on its standardization. The working method of OMG is based on making appeals for the submission of technologies; two products have been proposed: OLE2 and OpenDoc. OLE2 has been previously described, let us look at the main characteristics of OpenDoc.

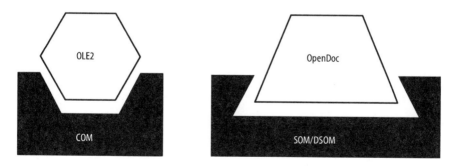

Fig 6.4 The two principal environments for handling composite documents.

6.3.1 OpenDoc

OpenDoc is a technology which allows the handling of composite documents. This technology was developed by Apple which then formed a consortium with IBM, Novell, Oracle, Taligent, SunSoft, WordPerfect and Xerox in order to port it onto a number of platforms. Today, OpenDoc runs on OS/2 and Macintosh. Versions for Windows-NT and AIX are at beta test stage. This consortium incorporates other technologies in support of OpenDoc. The two principal ones are:

- SOM and DSOM.[2] These two technologies come from IBM and represent the implementation of the CORBA standard. They allow communication between objects residing on the same machine or on two different machines. Thus objects in OpenDoc are based on the CORBA model and make use of its inter-machine communication protocols.

- Bento[3] container objects. This technology for storing documents comes from Apple. A file is a container that can hold document objects, each object being able, itself, to contain several versions of the data. Bento offers a set of functions which allow the efficient manipulation of documents.

6.3.2 The Standard for the Handling of Composite Documents

OMG, not surprisingly, in March 1996 adopted a standard very close to OpenDoc. It is called the *OMG Distributed Document Component Facility*. This standard is different from OpenDoc, by the fact that it does not use SOM functions and, in particular, its libraries, but uses the services already defined by OMG. As a result, the applications written conforming to the standard cannot operate with OpenDoc and vice versa. Note also that OpenDoc runs with SOM/DSOM to use CORBA objects. Currently, the ORB tools from different constructors are still not compatible, so it is necessary to wait for a further time (at best until the end of 1997) to have a real multi-vendor environment associated with OpenDoc.

Today, the market uses two technologies:

- OpenDoc, which must be slightly modified in order to satisfy the OMG standard, and which is based on a powerful object model (CORBA);

- OLE2, a non-standard product based on the COM object model, is already used to a considerable extent, and it represents a key technology for Microsoft.

Users will have to choose between these two technologies.

---

[2] SOM and DSOM are two trademarks of IBM. SOM stands for System Object Model, and DSOM stands for Distributed System Object Model.
[3] Bento are Japanese plates composed of several compartments which contain different kinds of food.

6.4   Bridge between CORBA and DCOM

It appears, after analysing the CORBA and DCOM models, that one is not better than the other, but that each has advantages with respect to the other. In this context, the best way ahead for a software constructor is not to choose between them, but to offer a bridge between the two. This bridge must allow an object from the DCOM world to communicate with an object from the CORBA world and vice versa.

DCOM and CORBA are also distinguished by the applications they support. Thus, in the document handling domain, COM forms the base for OLE, and CORBA forms that for OpenDoc. At this level, OLE seems to have taken a decisive advantage over OpenDoc because of the greater number of its users. However, OLE only runs today on a very limited type of machine (mainly Windows). Microsoft is currently trying to fill this gap by porting OLE to UNIX, IBM MVS and OpenVMS servers. As we have already seen, the distributed version of OLE is called DCOM. It seems reasonable to hope for the availability of DCOM on around 20 platforms at the end of 1997. For its part, CORBA is today available on many platforms because of the variety of existing products.

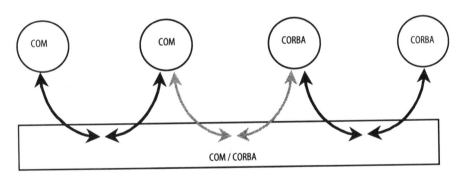

Fig 6.5 Complete inter-operability between COM and CORBA objects.

Following from these observations, the Digital Equipment Corporation offers its own tool, called ObjectBroker (which conforms to the CORBA standard) as a bridge to the OLE world. It allows a COM object to communicate with a CORBA object. The COM interface in ObjectBroker v2.6 acts at the level of OLE API and transforms COM calls into CORBA messages. Some restrictions are currently imposed on the protocol for communication between COM and CORBA objects. The final goal is to obtain COM objects that can talk in the same way between themselves or to CORBA objects and vice versa.

6.5 Summary Table

	CORBA	DCOM
Object	Multiple interfaces implemented using inheritance.	Multiple interfaces implemented via aggregation.
	Uses references to identify objects.	Only access to the interfaces of an object is possible.
		All OLE objects have the *IUnknown* interface
Interface	Is defined in the CORBA IDL language.	Is defined currently in Microsoft IDL (MIDL). MIDL must become a superset of CORBA IDL.
	Multiple APIs exist to activate operations: the dynamic API (DII) and the static API using a stub.	The *IUnknown* interface allows access to other interfaces.
Client	Is a program, not necessarily an object.	Is in general an OLE object.
	Communicates with the server object via the intermediary Object Request Broker (ORB).	Access to the server object can use RPC.
Object implementation	Is composed of the object adapter and code for methods.	Is composed of the code associated with each of the operations belonging to the interface.
	Allows the creation of references to objects.	
Communication	Inter-operability of products will only be possible with version 2.0.	DCE RPC will form the inter-system communication protocol.

7. *Internet and Middleware*

The aim of this chapter is to show that the combination of Internet and middleware technologies can lead to very interesting distributed application architectures. In particular, every new or existing application can be implemented on the Internet and thus become accessible throughout the entire world.

7.1 Introduction to the Internet

The Internet universe, also called cyberspace, is a network of networks whose nodes are computers. This universe was created in 1969 as the ARPANET project financed by the US Department of Defense. Its goal was to define new network technologies allowing a small group of researchers and administrators to share information. No notion of security was included since the goal was to obtain maximum access to data. The fact that more than 30 million users today share this universe has changed this original assumption. For a long time, the network of networks remained the province of academics and scientists. The trigger was pulled in 1993 when new software tools made the transfer of multimedia documents (text, images, video, sound) extremely easy. The contribution made by these new technologies was to lead to a new form of Internet which was to become known as the World Wide Web (WWW).

To connect to the Internet, the user must have a personal computer or a workstation. The connection can be direct or indirect. The connection is direct when using an already connected local network (LAN); this method is generally used inside a company. The connection is often indirect by using a telephone line and calling the number of a service provider who offers a connection to the network.

The Internet is characterized by the fact that it uses a unique communications protocol called TCP/IP (Transmission Control Protocol/Internet Protocol).

7.1.1 Definition of the Principal Terms

7.1.1.1 *Machine Naming*

Each computer belonging to the network has a unique IP (Internet Protocol) address. An IP address is 32 bits long and is composed of two elements: a network

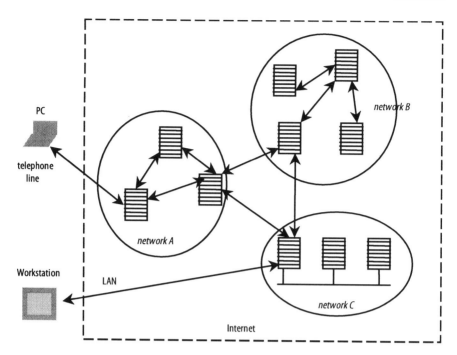

Fig 7.1 The Internet is a network of networks.

identifier and a machine identifier. It takes the form of four bytes with decimal values, for example, 16.36.155.19. People are not good with numbers, so names are used to denote machines. In order to convert a name into is numerical representation, a distributed database is available and used by the name conversion system; it is called a DNS – Domain Name System.

A machine name is organized as a list of domains separated by full stops (e.g. www.digital.com). Each domain represents a subset of the network and can itself be decomposed into sub-domains. A name can therefore contain as many domains as necessary. Name administration is not centralized but distributed. An administrative entity is responsible at the level of a domain. Thus, each group can create or change the names inside their domain.

The rules acting on the name structure are as follows:

- The part that is furthest to the right of the name represents either American entities or country codes. For example:

  .com   American commercial companies

  .edu   American educational organizations (universities, colleges, etc)

  .gov   American government

  .us   USA

  .fr   France

  .uk   United Kingdom

- The leftmost part is the name of a system or an alias.

- Between these two ends can appear as many domains as necessary.

Thus, the name *www.digital.com* represents an American commercial company whose domain name is "digital" and whose system is compatible with the World Wide Web (WWW or simply, the Web).

7.1.1.2 Internet Protocols

The first services offered on the Internet were of three types:

- inter-machine data transfer;
- remote user access to a machine;
- database access.

These different types of access use the following protocols:

- File Transfer Protocol (FTP). This protocol allows the transfer of files between remote machines. One can either read or copy a file to another machine.

- Telnet. This protocol allows connection to a remote machine and starting a session just as if one were a local user.

- Serial Line Internet Protocol (SLIP) and Point-to-Point Protocol (PPP). SLIP and PPP are standards for use with modems. SLIP allows access to the Internet via a fast modem and traditional telephone line. PPP is replacing SLIP.

- Wide Area Information Service (WAIS).The amount of data on the Internet is so great that index tables have been created in order to make access to them easier. These tables contain words which are associated with the addresses of the files where they appear. These tables are stored in databases whose access has been standardized. Archie is a database of this sort.

- Gopher. Gopher is a tool that allows the user to travel over the network using menus to access information. Gopher does not manipulate multi-media data itself but establishes links between the data appearing in the menus and the files containing them.

- World Wide Web (WWW). This is a more elaborate version of Gopher. It uses menus containing hypertext and allows the use of any sort of data (e.g., graphics, audio, etc.) The connections it uses allow uniform access to different services: FTP, Gopher, Telnet, WAIS, etc.

- HyperText Transfer Protocol (HTTP). This is a protocol pertaining only to the Web. It allows the transfer of multi-media documents.

- Intranet. An Intranet is a network that is owned entirely by a company and constructed using the same technologies as those on the Internet. Access to this network is protected. It offers all the functions of the Internet such as electronic mail, access to business information or file transfer. It also allows access to applications internal to the company.

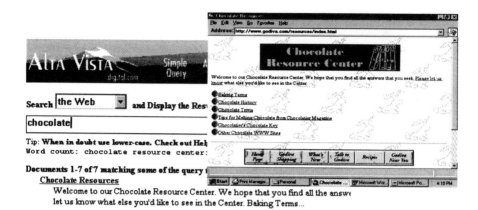

Fig 7.2 Hypertext example. "Chocolate Resources" is a hyperlink to another hypertext document.[1]

The World Wide Web is what has made the Internet popular. It has helped its use. This makes it worth looking at in more detail.

7.1.2 The World Wide Web

The World Wide Web is formed of a gigantic set of data that is distributed across the network in the form of hypertext and hypermedia documents. It also includes software providing access to this data. The software allowing navigation through the Web is called a Web browser or navigator.

A hypertext document contains text as well as links to other documents. These links are sometimes called hyperlinks. When the document is retrieved using a browser, the hyperlinks appear as words or groups of words that are underlined or coloured (or both). The act of clicking on a hyperlink triggers access to the document associated with it, and causes it to be displayed on the screen.

A hypermedia document is a hypertext document in which some connections point to documents containing images, sound, animation, etc.

7.1.2.1 Web Clients and Web Servers

A Web client is a piece of software which allows either interactive access (it operates, therefore, as a browser) or the execution of other user functions such as the construction of an index in order to accelerate access to information by browsers.

Current browsers are able to display text pages, images contained in these pages, and to play sound as well as video. In order to animate pages, there is also the

---

[1] This figure has been borrowed from a report entitled "Internet and distributed applications: describe sounded architectures to build applications over the internet" by Claude Falguière, April 1996.

possibility of incorporating little programs into the displayed document. These programs are activated by the browser when the page to which they belong is displayed.

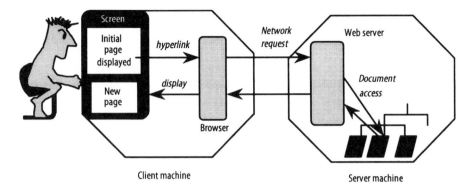

Fig 7.3 Access path to an Internet document.

A Web server is mainly a file server. The server knows how to decode the address sent by the client and will allow it to access the designated document. This document is transmitted to the client via the network. The server is able to encode the data which it sends over the network.

A server can also call applications or access databases.

7.1.2.2 Standard Elements of the Web

The Web offers many services (file transfers, electronic mail, document exchange) and in order to facilitate their implementation a certain number of standards have been defined. The current standards are GIF for images and MPEG for video.

The text documents that are exchanged are described in a standardized format called HTML (hypertext markup language). The fact that they circulate on a network has led to the definition of a network protocol called HTTP (hypertext transfer protocol) which is particularly suited to the transfer of multimedia documents. Access to different documents via different protocols has led to the standardization of the way in which documents are named. Thus, the URL (uniform resource locator) used to designate a file allows the identification of the machine, the protocol being used and the document localname.

Servers must be able to access applications or databases. To this end, a standard interface has been defined. It is called CGI (common gateway interface) and allows the activation of programs that are external to the server.

Uniform Resource Locator (URL)

To be accessible over the Web, every entity must have a URL. The URL associated with a document is unique and forms the access key used by clients (e.g., browsers). However the user does not always need to know the URL of a document to which they want to gain access. This address can be associated with a hyperlink in a page of text and thus hidden from the user. Here are some examples of a URL:

    http://home.netscape.com/index.html
    ftp://ftp.netscape.com/pub/
    news://news.announce.newusers

The structure of a URL consists of three elements. The first element specifies the network protocol. The second element represents the machine (see section 7.1.1.1). The third element indicates the address in the domain of the entity that is being sought (Fig 7.4).

Fig 7.4 Structure of a URL.

Uniform Resource Name (URN)

Access to a resource that is in great demand can incur an overhead on the network. In order to reduce the traffic, such a resource can be copied to several servers. The concept of a URN allows the designation of this resource and access to the nearest copy on the network to the client. A URN defines a resource in a unique fashion and it is possible that, in the future, browsers will use URNs more than URLs. In this case, a piece of software will allow the conversion of a URN into the URL of the nearest copy or the most easily accessible one on the network.

Uniform Resource Characteristics (URC)

The concept of a URC has, as its aim, that of offering information relative to a resource or to a document. This information can be of any kind: name of the document's author, expiry date for borrowed software, usage rights, price, etc.

7.1.2.3 HTML Standard

The HTML language separates the aspect of presentation from the aspect of content. During the creation of a document, the author must describe the content, the structural elements (e.g., title, paragraphs, chapters, etc.) as well as the description of its appearance (e.g., font, colour, etc). The final aspect of the document on the screen is entirely generated by the Web client (the browser). It is the client that decides the way in which the title or a chapter heading is displayed as a function of the information provided by the document. Thus, two different browsers can render the same document in different ways.

HTML is composed of hyperlinks. That is, references between documents or between components of documents. The interpreter of the language allows navigation along these links. A HTML document is composed of a list of elements delimited by tags at the start and end. For example, the tags <H1> and </H1> delimit the first level heading. These elements can be nested inside each other.

HTML has been used over the Web network since 1990. Different versions of this language exist, the last in date being HTML3. This is an object-oriented language which was designed in order to be able to be automatically generated by software such as text processors. This approach, which is the most common, leads to a minimization in the interest in learning to program this language which, similar to PostScript,[2] is used in a way that is transparent to the user.

A HTML document consists of a header and a body, and must include a title. Figure 7.5 shows an example of such a document with its graphical aspect.

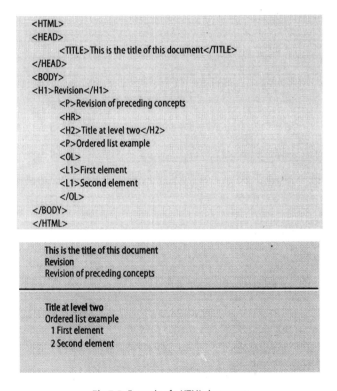

Fig 7.5 Example of a HTML document.

Link/Hyperlink

A link or hyperlink is a connection from one page to another, from one page to another part of the same page, or from a page to a label in another document. When a HTML page is displayed, links are represented by coloured words or groups of words in bold characters or in underlined characters. Figure 7.6 shows how a HTML link is coded and how the page appears on the user's screen.

---

[2] PostScript is a standard language used to describe documents to be printed.

```
<HTML>
<BODY>
<P>This paragraph contains a link to an anchor point whose name is anchor and which is situated
    in the same document as this text. <A HREF="#anchor">Go to this anchor</A>
<P>This paragraph contains a link to another HTML document whose name is OtherDocument.
<A HREF="http//www.company.com/otherdocument.htm">Go to OtherDocument</A>
<HR>
<P>...<P>...
<HR>
<P><A NAME="#anchor"></A>This is the anchor point called anchor
</BODY>
</HTML>
```

This paragraph contains a link to an anchor point whose
name is anchor and which is situated in the same document as this text.
Go to this anchor
This paragraph contains a link to another HTML document
whose name is OtherDocument. Go to OtherDocument

...

...

This is the anchor point called anchor

Fig 7.6 Example coding of a connection.

The images and icons whose borders are coloured also serve as links (Fig 7.7).

```
<BODY>
<AHREF=http://www.mycompany.com/aboutus.htm><IMG
SRC="aboutus.gif"></A> Click on this icon to get more information
about us
</BODY>
```

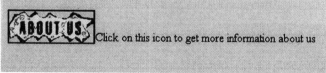

Click on this icon to get more information about us

Fig 7.7 Icon acting as a link.

Other types of links allow the transfer of software, of sound or of film. When a link of this type is activated, a file is downloaded and the application which allows its performance is activated. For example, if a text file created with MS-Word (so the name of the file ends with .doc) is transferred, the MS-Word application is automatically launched.

```
<BODY>
    <P>
    <A HREF="TextFile.doc">Load a MS Word document.</A>
</BODY>
```

Fig 7.8 Hyperlink allowing the activation of MS-Word software.

Insertion of Images in a HTML Document

There are two ways to insert an image into a HTML document. Either the image is an integral part of the document, or just its address appears in the document and the image is associated using a hyperlink. In the first case, the image appears at the same time as the rest of the document. In the second case, it is necessary to click on the hyperlink to make it appear. Figure 7.9 shows the code associated with an image integrated with a document, while Figure 7.10 shows the way to write a hyperlink in HTML code.

```
<BODY>
    <H1>An inline Image</H1>
    <IMG SRC="imagename.gif">>
</BODY>
```

Fig 7.9 Example of an image belonging to a document.

```
<BODY>
    <A HREF="imagename.gif"> <H1>A link to an external image</H1></A>
</BODY>
```

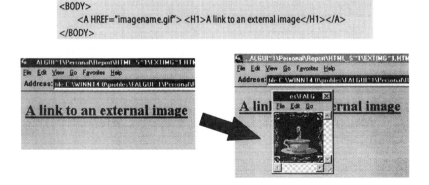

Fig 7.10 Example of an image associated with a hyperlink.

7.1.2.4   The HTTP Protocol

The HTTP protocol allows communication between a Web client and a server to be structured. The dialogue runs as follows:

- The client takes the initiative in the dialogue and, using a URL, connects to a Web server.

- In its request, the client specifies a name of a method indicating the operation that is desired. The current methods are:

  o *get.* If the designated resource is a file or a document, the *get* method obtains its contents. If it is a matter of a program or a script, the *get* method passes it some parameters, requests its execution and the data which result from its execution.

  o *post.* This method is similar to the *get* method, but is recommended for the transfer of data from the client to the server. This data comes from a form in HTML and can be passed to the destination in many ways.

  o *put* or *delete.* These methods allow the creation, modification or deletion of server resources.

- The server replies by sending a state code, a header and the contents of the document if it is available.

- The end of connection is executed by the client or by the server.

A HTML page can contain images. When such a page is sent by the server, it does not directly contain images but their addresses (URLs). The client's browser must connect to the URL associated with each image in order to download it. To accelerate the downloading of a document containing many images, a browser can be made to open several connections at the same time.

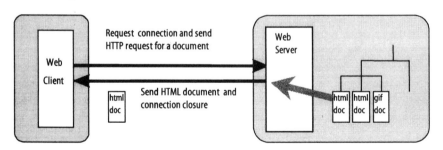

Fig 7.11 Structure of the HTTP protocol.

Handling Data Associated with a Form

HTML pages can be used to capture data in order to transmit it to an application or to a database. A form is the HTML page component which allows the capture of data from a screen. Figure 7.12 shows the code for a form and its graphical representation on the screen. The graphics associated with the above sequence of code is shown in Figure 7.13.

```
<HTML>
<BODY>
    <FORM METHOD="POST" Action="http//www.company.com/example">
<P>Name: <INPUT NAME="Name">
<P>Surname: <INPUT NAME="Surname">
<P><INPUT TYPE=SUBMIT><INPUT TYPE=RESET>
</FORM>
</BODY>
    </HTML>
```

Fig 7.12 Example code describing a form in a HTML page.

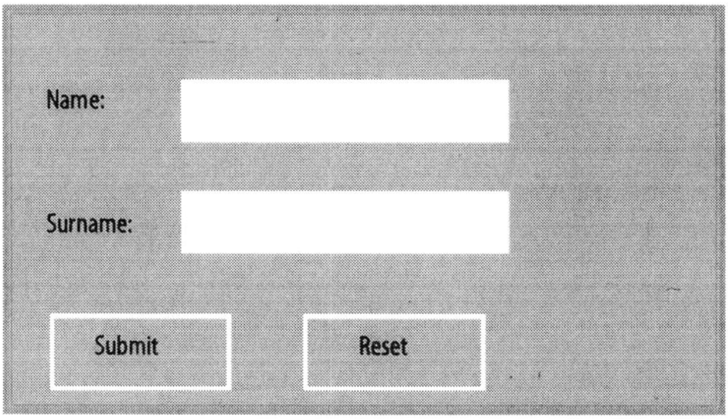

Fig 7.13 Graphic representing the form described in Figure 7.12.

The data entered by the user are captured at the HTML page level and formatted by the browser to be transmitted to the server. The browser constructs a string of characters containing the name of the input fields as well as their values, that is, the text typed by the user. The format of this string obeys the following rules:

1. Each pair (attribute, value) is coded as follows: attribute=value (for example, Name=Christian);

2. If a value contains a space or the character "&" then the space character is replaced by the sign "+" and the character "&" by its ASCII code expressed as a hexadecimal number (for example, Name=Daniel+Martin Surname=D%26M);

3. Pairs (attribute, value) are separated by the symbol "&" (for example, Name=Daniel+Martin&Surname=D%26M).

The complete structure of the message that is sent to the web server contains three parts: the name of the method used (*get* or *post*), the URL, and the string holding the parameters. In the example shown in Figure 7.12, the complete message that is transmitted (assuming that the *post* method is used, and that the name is Daniel Martin and the surname is D&M) is:

post
http://www.company.com/example?Name=Daniel+Martin&Surname=D%26M

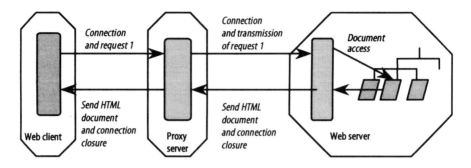

Fig 7.14 The proxy server filter's access to the Web server.

Proxy Server

The concept of a proxy server was introduced in order to manage access to Web servers. The proxy server lives on a machine that is different from the one containing the Web server, and its main aim is to filter requests for connections (firewall). It also provides other functions such as the conversion of documents from one format to another. Typically, the client connects to it and makes its request to the proxy server which transmits it to the Web server after verification. The server returns the document requested by the client to the proxy server which then sends it to the client (see Fig 7.14).

Differences between the FTP and HTTP Protocols

The table below indicates the primary differences between the two data transfer protocols FTP and HTTP.

FTP	HTTP
Two-way connection: the client connects to the server to make their request and the server connects to the client in order to send the requested file.	One-way connection
The server maintains a connection state. It also records the results of previous requests.	No state is kept. All the information used by the server is in the request. The reply must be contained in a single message.
Does not know of the file type being manipulated.	Information necessary to the server (file type, browser type) appears in the header of a HTTP request.

HTTP and Security

The dialogue between a client and a server on the Web is not in general protected against dishonest intervention. It is possible to tap into such a conversation and to obtain the information exchanged between client and server. This implies that sensitive data, such as passwords and credit card numbers, should not be allowed to circulate through the Web without protection. In order to be able to exchange such information, there now exist servers which use coding techniques for data and for client identification.

Thus, a URL which starts with the string *https://* instead of *http://* indicates that the document is coming from a protected server. In the same way, a URL which begins with *snews:* instead of *news:* indicates that the document comes from a protected news server.

7.1.2.5 CGI: Interface between a Web Server and an Application

A server on the Web can offer functions other than those of a file server. Thus, when it receives a URL, instead of returning the contents of the desired file, it can treat this file as a program and execute it. It then returns the data generated by the program in the form of a HTML page. The way in which the server activates the program and passes its parameters to it forms the CGI standard.

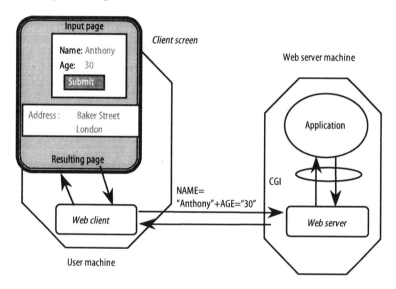

Fig 7.15 Connection between a Web server and an application using CGI.

This scheme requires that a HTML page contains fields to gather data and a special button called "submit" with which is associated the URL of the program to execute. The user must first enter their data in the HTML page on display, then click on the submit button. The data is then given a HTTP format (attribute-value pairs, for example NAME="Anthony"+AGE="30") and sent to the server. The server updates certain environment variables, runs the program passing to it the user's data either using the QUERY_STRING variable or via the standard input stream (stdin). When the program has finished its processing, it sends the server the result in the form of a HTML page which is returned to the client (Fig 7.15).

Example CGI program: AltaVista[3]

Finding information on the Web can be an annoying task, given the enormous quantity of data that is available. In order to ease the task for the user, search tools

---

[3] AltaVista is a registered trademark of Digital Equipment Corporation.

have been implemented. AltaVista is the most famous and the most powerful of them. AltaVista allows the description of areas of interest and returns the list of documents that refer to it.

For example, if one enters "apple pie" as the domain of interest, and clicks on the submit button, a request is sent to the server which transfers it to the AltaVista CGI program using the QUERY_STRING variable. This program searches in its database for references to apple pie, incorporates them into a HTML document which it returns to the server. The server transmits this document to the client which originally issued the request.

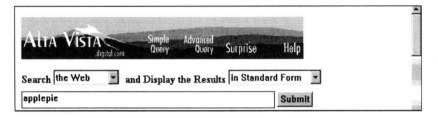

Fig 7.16 Alta Vista, a powerful tool for searching the Web for information.

7.2   Internet Architectures

The aim of this chapter is to analyze the different architectures which integrate Web technologies with those concerning middleware. For each of them, the advantages and disadvantages are stated.

7.2.1 File Servers

The traditional architecture used in the Web combines a client and a server (Fig 7.17). The user either directly or indirectly (using hyperlinks) provides the address (URL) of a document using a browser which transmits it to the appropriate server. This server accesses the document which belongs to the local file store and transfers it to the Web client which displays it. It will be observed that the file can contain any data format, the most common being the HTML language.

This architecture is well appropriate for the broadcast of information inside (intranet) or outside (Internet) a company to the extent that it is accessible anywhere and from any type of machine.

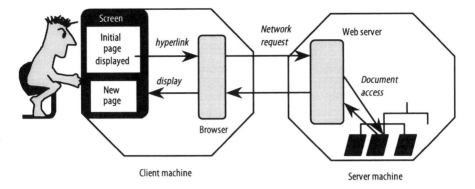

Fig 7.17 Architecture of a Web server for files.

7.2.2 CGI Application Server

In this architecture, the address (URL) makes reference to a file that does not contain data to be displayed but a program. This file is stored in a directory (e.g., /cgi-bin). When a request to such a file is received, the server does not send it to the client, but starts its execution and gathers the result in order to send them to the client. If this result must be displayed the program generates it with a HTML format.

In order to be able to pass parameters to the program, the HTML language offers the possibility of describing the information-gathering fields stored in a page. The data provided by the user is recovered by the browser which sends them to the server (see section 7.1.2.5). The way in which the server communicates with the application is formalized and is called CGI. Applications (also CGI programs) are very often written in scripting languages such as PERL and TCL. However, nothing stops one from writing them in other languages (for example, C++).

This approach is very commonly used on the Web due to its simplicity, but it does have a number of disadvantages:

- The CGI program is started at every request, that is, each time that a browser makes a reference to it and stops after completion of the request. The starting of an executable program is costly in processing time and this load translates to the user as longer response times.

- The logical connection between the browser and the server has a duration and a life which is that of the request. It is established for each request and ends with it. The establishment of the connection represents an additional cost which also increases the response time.

- The Web server does not save any context related to a request coming from a browser. This means that every request to a CGI program is handled in isolation. This is acceptable while the amount of data to return is limited but it is no longer acceptable if it is a matter of running over a long list in order to gain some information. Let us imagine the example of where the user is looking for Mr Martin in a telephone number database for the London region. It is highly probable that several hundred replies are possible. It is plausible that the CGI program accessing this database, returns a small number of responses (perhaps the first 20). If the person being looked up does not appear in this list, the user must be able to tell the CGI program to continue its search starting from the place where it was stopped. This implies that the search context is retained somewhere.

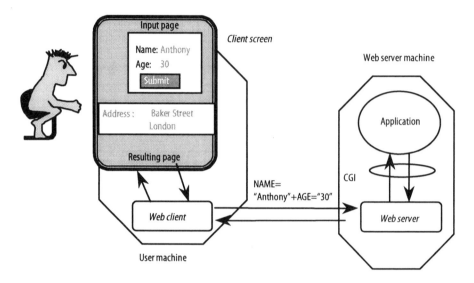

Fig 7.18 Architecture of an application CGI server.

In order to solve these problems, a certain number of solutions have been proposed and implemented. They are described in the following subsections.

7.2.3 CGI Architectures with Context Saving

In order to make the dialogue between a browser and a Web server more efficient, a certain number of solutions have been implemented. They are presented in increasing order of efficiency.

7.2.3.1 The Concept of a Hidden Field

The concept of a hidden field allows the context of the CGI program to be stored in the browser. The HTML language defines forms which allow data entered by the user to be collected. Among these forms, there is a special one which is hidden from the user but which allows the storage of data.

In the example given above, for a search for Mr Martin, the HTML page contains the name of Mr Martin in a data-gathering form, and in a display form, the list of the 20 replies that were returned by the CGI program via the Web server. The last name in the list can then be stored in a hidden form in the HTML page. When the user presses the "next" button, to obtain the next 20 names on the list, the browser sends the CGI program the name which indicates the place from which it must restart its search.

This approach works properly, but it is always considered to be inefficient and, above all, inelegant.

7.2.3.2 The Concept of "Cookies"

The Netscape company has suggested another solution to the problem of saving the context of a CGI application at the browser level. In this solution, the CGI program groups the information to be saved by the browser in an object called a *cookie*, and it is the responsibility of the browser to return the cookie to the program to which it is making the next request (see Fig 7.19).

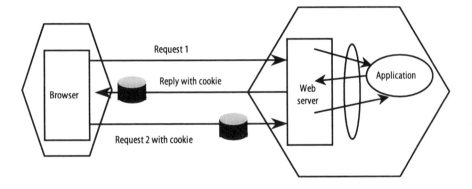

Fig 7.19 Backup of context in a cookie.

The main difference between the hidden field and the cookie methods lies in the fact that cookies are stored outside of the HTML page. From this fact, the data contained in a cookie can be more protected and can have a life of their own. The disadvantage is that this concept is not standard and its implementation is left to the good will of the constructors of Web browsers and servers.

7.2.3.3 The Concept of a Context File

In order to reduce the amount of context information exchanged between Web client and server, another possibility is to store such information in a file local to the server. Thus, when a CGI program is activated for the first time, it returns the data (or a part of the data) required to the server and stores its context in a file. The name of the file is sent to the client either by the hidden field method, or by the cookie technique. When the second request comes, the browser must provide the name of the file which will then be transmitted to the CGI program.

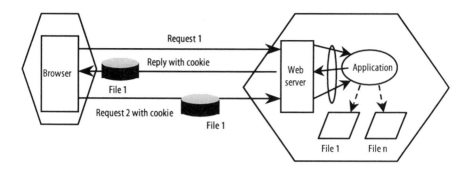

Fig 7.20 The context of a CGI program can be backed up to file.

The weakness of the CGI approach lies in the fact that the program must be restarted on each request. This led Web server constructors to offer an interface that allows the connection to an already active external program. Thus, the DLL technology under Windows and shared object technology under Unix offer the possibility of permanently loading a program into memory. To each of these programs is associated a URL and when this is referenced, the corresponding program is activated.

This domain is still bubbling with activity and each vendor suggests their own interface. Thus, Netscape offers NSAPI and Microsoft offers ISAPI. However, no standard more developed than CGI is available at the present time.

7.3   Putting an Application onto the Internet

One very important aspect of the Internet technology is allowing access from anywhere in the world to an application that is old or has been newly developed and is running on a machine connected to the network. This possibility offers new perspectives for companies because this approach works for existing applications as well as for new ones. The interest in this can be easily understood: every employee in a large company during their business trips can access their favourite applications from their hotel room. Whether this person is a manager, a lawyer or an engineer, they will have access to their working environment as if they were in their own office.

From the computing person's viewpoint, the approach is also interesting because it requires no modification or re-writing of existing applications which are required to be available on the network. It makes software version handling easier because the software exists in a single copy on the central machine instead of existing on all the user PCs.

The architectures which are now described show how, by combining Internet and middleware technologies, it is possible to integrate applications distributed over the Internet.

7.3.1 Integration and Wrapping

One way to make an existing application that has a dumb-terminal type of interface (e.g., IBM 3270 or VT) available on a PC is to emulate the terminal. This approach is commonly used in companies at present but it is extremely inconvenient. It overloads the network because the communication protocol is not optimized and does not improve the external appearance of the application in any way.

Another way of doing things is to use the technique of wrapping. This technique consists of "wrapping" the existing application in some additional software. This additional software knows how to communicate with the application in those ways required by the application's design and offers a new API (Application Programming Interface) to the outside world. It is then possible to develop a graphical environment for the client in terms of this new API. The result is a client–server structure in which the client is the new graphical interface and the server is the set formed from the wrapping software and the old application. In this new arrangement, the client and the server do not necessarily reside on the same machine (see Fig 7.21). This approach allows the development of a client which runs in a windowed environment (e.g., Windows) and making the best use of the facilities that the environment offers. The result of wrapping technology is that all the functions offered by the application have not changed, but the application interface becomes graphical and can operate remotely.

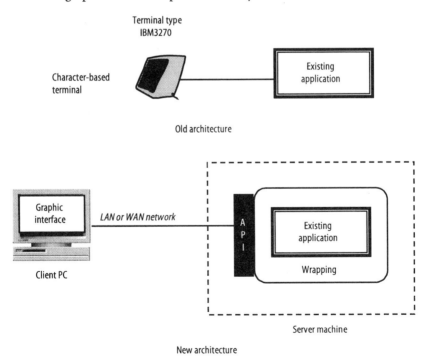

Fig 7.21 The wrapping technique.

7.3.2 Generic Architecture for a Web Application

The availability of an application over the Web assumes that this application has a client–server architecture. The client part is formed from the graphical interface written in the HTML language in order to be able to be displayed on a browser. The server part is connected to the Web server. The generic way to perform the integration of such an application on the Web is shown in Figure 7.22. Several versions exist and will be considered below. The activation and execution of such an application goes as follows (cf. Fig 7.22):

1. The user, at the browser, requests a HTML page (e.g., *page_i/f*) which forms the application's interface (❶).

2. The request travels across the network and arrives at the Web server (❷).

3. The Web server accesses the *page_i/f* page (❸).

4. The server returns the requested page to the browser (*page_i/f*) (❹).

5. The user sees the *page_i/f* page on their screen (❺). It forms the interface to the application. The user can then enter the data required by this application. When all the data has been entered, the user clicks on the submit button associated with this page in order to send the data to the application.

6. The data travels across the network in HTTP form (❻). This request also contains the name of the CGI program to activate.

7. The Web server activates the application and passes it the parameters (or data) (❼).

8. The application returns the results of its processing in HTML format to the Web server (❽).

9. The Web server transmits these results to the browser which displays them (❾).

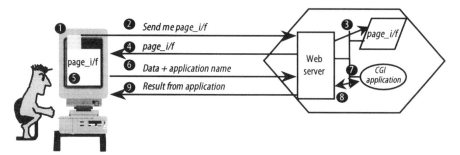

Fig 7.22 Architecture of an application on the Web.

It can be noted that the generic architecture is a combination of two Internet functions: the downloading of a HTML file and the execution of a CGI program. The inherent limitations of the CGI program have already been discussed (section 7.2.2). Below, we will describe the existing solutions to these limitations.

7.3.3 Architectures Integrating an Old Application

The term "old application" must be made more precise. It means, in this context, an application that has already been written and whose code is not to be rewritten. This application can be old to the company and the source code cannot be modified for whatever reason. It can be an application that has been newly purchased whose source code is unavailable.

The generic architecture model requires that the application contains code to support the CGI protocol. This is clearly impossible for an old application. Its integration leads to the use of the wrapping technique. It is then necessary to develop a CGI module providing two functions:

1. exchange information with the Web server;

2. communicate this data to the application proper using its API. The architecture that finally results is shown in Figure 7.23.

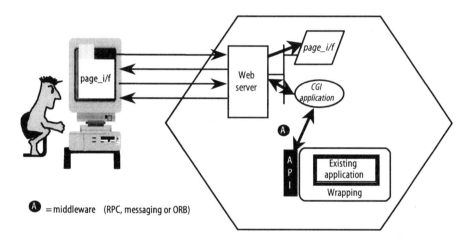

Fig 7.23 Architecture integrating an old application.

In this architecture, the CGI module must communicate with the old application which has been wrapped. This can be implemented by middleware such as RPC, message-based middleware or object-based middleware (CORBA or COM). Thus use of middleware removes the constraint that the old application must reside on the same machine as the Web server. This can then lead to an architecture in which the Web server and CGI module run on one machine and the old application on another.

This architecture evolves as a function of the middleware that is used. To convince ourselves of this approach, let us consider the example discussed in the following section in which an object-based middleware of the CORBA type is used.

7.3.4 Architecture Integrating an Application using Object-based Middleware

In the example considered here (Fig 7.24), the application that we want to put on the Web is composed of distributed objects that communicate via the intermediary of CORBA middleware. The interesting thing about this technology is that the CGI module can also play the role of a client with respect to the object servers and can be attached to the middleware. The connection between the Web server and the object bus in the application is then easily implemented.[4]

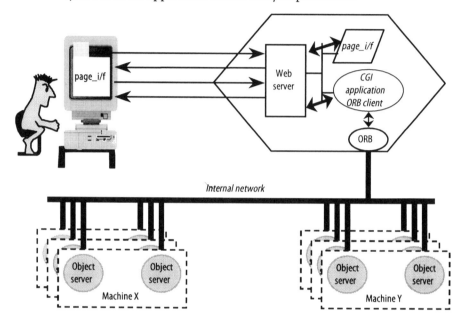

Fig 7.24 Integration of an application on the Internet using object-based middleware.

The power of this architecture lies in the fact that it offers access across the Internet to resources that are distributed on the company's internal network. Assuming all of a company's applications are implemented using objects connected to a single bus, this architecture allows access to them via the Internet, that is, from anywhere in the world. Elementary protection measures are always needed to prevent unauthorized access.

Such an architecture exists today. It is simple to manage and consists of many applications. The response times are adequate when the amount of information that is exchanged is not excessive. However, when the number of users becomes large, performance degradation occurs. This is due to the nature of the HTTP protocol and to the fact that there must exist one CGI instance per user.

---

[4] This model can be implemented using the ObjectBroker middleware tool from Digital Equipment Corporation.

7.3.5 Architecture Using Intelligent Clients

The great interest in Internet technology is that it offers access to a network that encompasses the entire world. However, some of these technologies do not provide a level of performance that is acceptable for some types of application or user. This is particularly the case for the HTTP protocol and for the HTML language. One approach has been proposed which allows the application to free itself of HTTP during its execution and offers a graphic interface of greater quality. This approach suggests, during downloading of a HTML page that is part of the application's interface, to download the code as well. This way of doing things has two advantages:

1. It executes on the client machine and ensures the connection with the CORBA object bus by means of the use of the Internet Inter-ORB Protocol (IIOP). Thus the dialogue between the HTML interface and the rest of the application no longer uses the HTTP protocol.

2. It also allows the introduction in the interface of new functions such as data validation or the dynamic addition of graphical elements.

It is a characteristic of the Internet that everything that executes on the client must be able to execute on any machine at all (the concept of portability). This is a characteristic of the HTML language, and must be a characteristic of downloaded code. This is why a new language called JAVA (introduced by Sun Microsystems Inc.) was defined for writing this source. Java is very close to the C++ language. It offers, among other things, a set of classes allowing Internet connections, TCP/IP, and HTML document processing. To be executed, Java requires the existence of an interpreter on the client machine. Java code fragments which have been transferred across the Internet are called *applets*.

The network protocol used by the World Wide Web (HTTP) and the network protocol used by CORBA have, as a common subset, the IIOP protocol. IIOP defines a standard representation for CORBA data for their transmission over the network and describes in detail mechanisms for message exchange at the TCP/IP level.

The introduction of Java technology allows, in addition to a substantial improvement in interface quality, the design of new architectures such as those shown in Figure 7.25. In this architecture, the operating sequence is as follows:

1. The user from their browser requests the HTML page (e.g, *page_i/f*) which forms the interface to the application and which contains the reference to the file containing Java code.

2. The request travels across the network and arrives at the Web server.

3. The Web server accesses the page *page_i/f*.

4. The server returns the requested page (*page_i/f*) to the browser.

5. The browser displays the page *page_i/f* which forms the application's interface. In the HTML code, there is a reference to the Java applet.

6. The browser requests the server to get the file containing the Java applet to be sent.

7. When it receives the code, the browser begins its execution.

8. The applet execution is performed, thanks to the interpreter which must be present on the client machine.

9. The Java applet appears as a client to the CORBA ORB which resides on the client machine.

10. The CORBA ORB on the user machine communicates with the CORBA ORB on the server machine where all or part of the application objects reside.

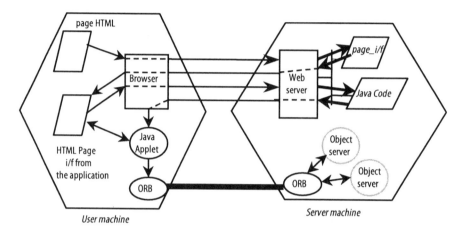

Fig 7.25 Java client communicating via object-based middleware.

The approach depicted in Figure 7.25 is valuable because it combines the advantages of Web and distributed object technologies. The Web is used to download a Java applet which forms the application's interface and which allows communication with the other components of this application via a middleware object. Such an architecture is implementable today, but only in the laboratory. No product which is fully worth the name is currently available on the market despite all the publicity about this concept. However, matters are rapidly developing in this area, and it can reasonably be hoped that in the near future, there will be industrial tools available that will provide these functions.

The example shown in Figure 7.25 uses CORBA middleware. In fact other middleware can be used. There exist Java classes which allow the use of RPC middleware or which can make TCP/IP requests.

7.3.6 Security via Virtual Private Networks: Intranet

A great weakness of the Internet is currently its lack of security. The problems associated with security can be decomposed into two large classes:

- To control access to a Web server. The goal here is only to accept requests coming from an authorized person. This control can be realized by the introduction of a piece of specific software called a *firewall*. This software generally runs on a machine that is different from the one containing the Web server in order to ensure perfect security. The network situated inside the firewall is protected and private and forms an Intranet network (Fig 7.26).

- To protect the data which circulate through the network. The goal here is to be able to exchange data in complete security, that is, without intrusion from a third person, between two machines that communicate over the Internet. One way to achieve this objective is to encrypt the data at the sender level and for the receiver to know how to decrypt them. To do this, the concept of a tunnel is employed. A tunnel is obtained by introducing a firewall at the level of the sender to ensure the encryption of the data and a firewall at the level of the receiver in order to perform the decryption of the data and to authorize the request. The network that is situated between these two client and server entities is the Internet. However, the fact that messages are protected by this tunnel effect leads to our considering this as a virtual network that belongs to the company which installed the firewalls on its two machines. This virtual network is called an *Intranet* (Fig 7.27).

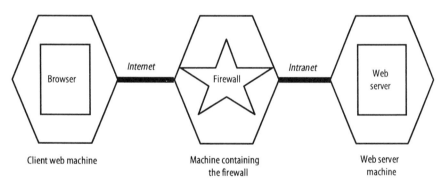

Fig 7.26 Protection of a Web server by a firewall.

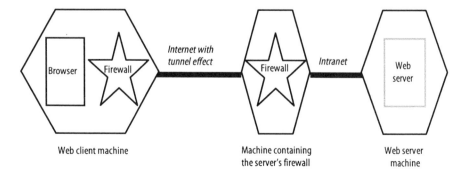

Fig 7.27 Concept of a private virtual network using the tunnel effect.

The technologies comprising the firewall are already available. Some existing industrial products are on the market. It is also necessary to observe that the security mechanisms described here can be combined with the architectures that we introduced above. The combination of all of these technologies leads to application architectures which are really distributed over networks that are simultaneously internal and external to the company.

8. *Java RMI and Java Beans*

The Java[1] language introduces new mechanisms allowing many ways to implement distributed objects. These new technologies run over the Internet and more generally over TCP/IP networks. They form a new generation of middleware tools which it is important to study. In this chapter, we describe the mechanisms for distribution in the Java language, but do not present the language itself.

8.1 The Java Language

The term "Java" originally denoted a new object-oriented programming language inspired by the C++ language and cleaned of certain functions which prevent portability (e.g., pointers). The major characteristic of the Java language is its portability, that is, its capacity to run on any platform. This is why the following phrase has become the Java emblem: 'Write Once, Run Anywhere™'.

The Java language was defined in order to write code that can be downloaded from a network onto any machine. This aim imposed a number of constraints of which the following are two:

- the code to be downloaded must also be as compact as possible in order to reduce network traffic;

- the Java language must be able to execute on any machine.

The first constraint was resolved by using an intermediate language called byte-codes or p-code. This language, already used in some third generation language compilers, is characterized by a minimal size and complete independence with respect to machine language. Thus, the code for a program written in Java is translated (or compiled) during its construction phase into the bytecode language. During the usage phase, it is the bytecodes that traverse the network.

The second constraint – that is, portability of Java programs – was solved using an interpreter for the bytecodes. This solution assumes that on each platform where Java programs are desired to execute, there is this interpreter. Thus, the bytecodes are not compiled (or translated) into machine code then executed, but interpreted, that is each instruction is compiled then executed.

---

[1] "Java" and the phrase "Java RMI" are registered trademarks of Sun Microsystems Inc.

In the case of the Internet[2] the user can download Java code, or more exactly the bytecodes. It is not then a matter of an application properly speaking, but of an application component which needs a browser to execute. This is why the term *applet* is used to denote these little program fragments.

Downloading code across the network can turn out to be a dangerous operation as far as the receiver is concerned. This is why a module verifies that the code that is received does not contain operations that can threaten the integrity of the machine (e.g., access to local disks).

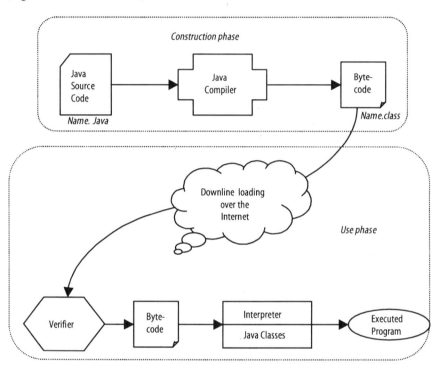

Fig 8.1 Production and use phases of a Java applet.

This operating scheme requires the existence on the receiving machine of an interpreter and a verification module. These two components belong to what is called the Java Virtual Machine (or JVM). This software machine is composed of a set of modules which we will consider in more detail later in this chapter (see section 8.3.4). Figure 8.1 shows the different steps followed by a program written in Java in order that it can be executed on any platform. They are:

1. Writing of the Java program. The name of the file containing the code has the *.java* extension.

2. Compilation of this program and the generation of bytecodes. The name of the file containing the bytecodes has the *.class* extension.

---

[2] Many terms pertaining to the Internet are used here; we recommend the reader who is unfamiliar with these terms to refer to Chapter 7.

3. Downloading of the bytecodes or applet.

4. Verification of the downloaded code.

5. Execution of the applet by the interpreter at the request of the browser.

8.2 Distributed Processing with Java

In order to reveal the new possibilities offered by the Java language, let us consider the very simple case of an application. Traditionally, an application performs some kind of processing of data. This implies that there are two parts which contain data and program code, respectively. The data can come, for example, from a database or a file. The application code having to process the data, it results that these two elements must be present on the same machine at the time processing occurs.

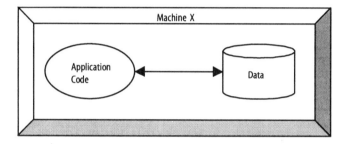

Fig 8.2 Processing model for an application and its data.

The fact that this application is distributed means that the code part and the data part reside on two different machines (see Fig 8.3(a)).

In order to allow the execution of this application, it is necessary to group the data and code on the same machine. Two approaches are now possible thanks to Java (see Fig 8.3(b)):

1. Transfer the data (❶) to the machine containing the application's code (let this be machine X in the example in Fig 8.3). This method has been available for a long time and has been implemented using many technologies called data middleware. The best known of these is Object Data Base Connectivity (ODBC).[3]

2. Transfer the code (❷) to the machine containing the data (say, machine Y in the example in Fig 8.3). This concept is now possible thanks to mechanisms offered by Java and developed in this chapter.

---

[3] ODBC is a Microsoft technology.

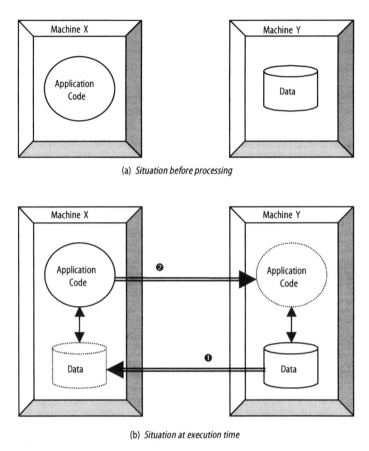

(a) *Situation before processing*

(b) *Situation at execution time*

Fig 8.3 Distributed application: transfer of data or transfer of code.

We have seen in previous chapters that distributed processing also means, and above all means, the decomposition of an application into several processing components. The nature of these components depends on the type of middleware that is used: for RPC technology, the components are procedures, for message queues, the components are applications, and for object-based middleware, the components are objects. In each of these middleware technologies, the components exchange data but in no case is a component itself transferred across the network. Thus, in Figure 8.4, object ① communicates with object ② by exchange of message. In this model, the code remains on the machine where it was installed. There is only data transfer. At the opposite extreme, Java also allows the transfer of processing. Thanks to Java an object can travel across the network and be passed from one object to another.

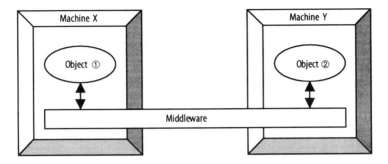

Fig 8.4 The object-based middleware bus transfers data between objects.

8.3   Internet: Downloading and Execution of Applets

8.3.1 Downloading an Application

Java and Internet are tightly coupled. The basic mechanism provided by the Internet consists of downloading files that are on remote machines (called servers) onto the user machine. The downloaded file is, if its type permits, displayed on the screen. This file can form the data gathering interface of an application and, to this end, can require the addition of specific processing. The sequence of code representing this processing is contained in a file that is also downloaded. This must be written in the Java language in order to execute on any machine. To do this, the file to be displayed (of type *.html*) contains a reference to the file containing the Java code (of type *.class*). This file will be downloaded when requested by the browser. The complete operating scheme is as follows (Fig 8.5):

- The user gives the address of the file of type *.html* that they want to see displayed on the screen (❶).

- The request from the user is interpreted by the browser which transmits it across the Internet network (❷). This request contains the address of the server machine where the desired file is stored.

- On the server machine there runs a piece of software called the Web server which receives the request containing the name of the file (❸).

- The Web server reads the file from the local disk and sends it to the user's browser (❹).

- The browser interprets the code in the *.html* file that has been received and displays it on the user's screen (❺).

- In the code in this file, the key-word "<APPLET>" occurs indicating the reference to a Java (*.class*) file (❻). Automatically, the browser generates a request asking for the downloading of this file. Figure 8.6 shows the case of a file called *example.html* containing a reference to an applet. The file containing the applet is called *Hello.class*.

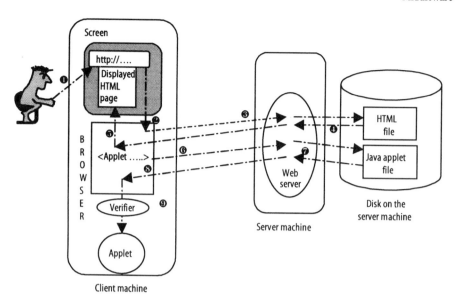

Fig 8.5 Loading a Java application.

- This request is received by the Web server which reads the file from the local disk (❼). This file contains the compiled (bytecode) Java code representing the applet.

- The Web server sends this *.class* file to the client's browser (❽). The browser notes that it is dealing with a *.class* file and loads it into the Java virtual machine.

- The applet is examined by the verification module in the Java virtual machine in order to ensure that it contains no illegal instruction (❾). Following this test, the applet is ready to run.

```
<HTML>
<HEAD>
    <TITLE>Very simple program
    </TITLE>
</HEAD>
<BODY>
    Call a Java applet :
    <APPLET CODE= "Hello.class"
        WIDTH=150 HEIGHT=25>
    </APPLET>
</BODY>
</HTML>
```

Fig 8.6 File example.html contains a reference to an applet.

In the **mechanism** that was described above, the data is found on the client machine and the code, represented by the applet, is downloaded using the Internet

HTTP protocol. This forms the first way to transfer code from one machine to another. Note that this transfer is started by the browser.

8.3.2 Execution of an Applet

The execution of an applet is started by the browser following a user action. In order to reduce the size of an applet to be transferred, only the main class is loaded. This is interpreted by the *Interpreter* module in the JVM and when a call to a missing class is performed, the JVM dynamically loads this class. This function is implemented by the *Loader* module in the JVM. This module searches to see if the class belongs to the local library. It this is not the case, the *Loader* sends a standard HTTP request in order to download the missing class (see Fig 8.7). This mechanism allows only classes useful to the given task to be loaded.

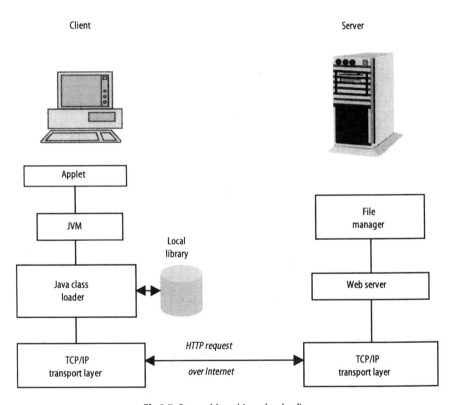

Fig 8.7 Demand-based Java class loading.

8.3.3 URL Connection

In the process described above, the request for downloading is initiated by the JVM. Another mechanism allows the applet itself to initiate such a request. This has the name *URL connection*.[4]

The combination of two Java instructions is necessary so an applet can download code. They are:

- The *URL(Specification)* instruction. This allows the establishment of a connection with the desired object. In the following example, a connection is first established with the file containing the class that is desired to be loaded (e.g., *object1.class*):

    URL url = new URL(www.company.com/object1.class)

- The *GetContent(url)* instruction. This allows the code of the object designated by the URL to be downloaded.

    GetContent(url)

The above call initializes the transfer of *object1.class*.

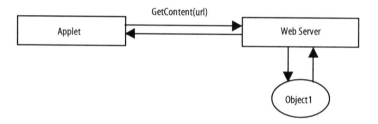

Fig 8.8 Request for the downloading of an object by an applet.

8.3.4 Structure of the Java Virtual Machine (JVM)

In order for the Java code to be executed on any platform, the platform must make a specific software environment available. This environment is made up of a set of modules which form what Sun calls the Java Virtual Machine (JVM). This is comprised of:

- The verifier. This module verifies that the downloaded code does not contain illegal instructions. In particular, it ensures that no local disk access is performed. It also verifies that only network requests are sent to the machine where the code came from.

- The interpreter. The Java code is interpreted locally by this module.

---

[4] URL stands for Uniform Resource Locator; see Chapter 7 for more details.

- The library. A certain number of Java classes manipulating standard objects are frequently used. In order to avoid downloading them, these classes are stored locally in this library.

- Native methods. Some operations (in particular graphics) are dependent on the platform on which the JVM runs. These operations are called native methods.

- The garbage collector. Java is an object-oriented language in which objects are created and then destroyed. The memory allocated to these objects during their creation must be freed when they are destroyed. The management of these "pieces" is the task performed by the garbage collector.

- The Just-In-Time (JIT) compiler. This component is optional and was proposed by the Digital Equipment Corporation. In order to increase the speed of execution of an applet, this module first performs compilation so as to avoid interpretation. Note that this possibility is only interesting if the code contains loops or is executed several times. Measurements have shown that on average the use of such a compiler can speed processing by a factor of 20.

This JVM machine runs on top of an operating system (e.g., Windows95 or UNIX) and uses a browser (also called a navigator). Thus, these are the three components necessary and sufficient for an Internet platform: the browser, the JVM and the operating system (see Fig 8.9).

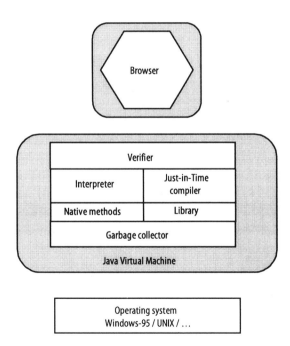

Fig 8.9 Internet platform and Java virtual machine.

8.4   Remote Method Invocation: Java RMI

Remote method call in Java allows objects belonging to one Java virtual machine (JVM) to transparently invoke methods belonging to objects in another JVM. This is no different from the CORBA model for activating remote methods. The originality of the Java RMI comes from the fact that the call parameters to an object can be themselves Java objects. Thus Java objects can be spread across the Internet or any TCP/IP network. In the CORBA processing model, objects are not mobile. The main reason being that their code is not portable. Java code being able to execute on any platform, every object written in Java can circulate through the network in order to be executed on the machine best suited to current conditions.

The Java RMI uses the technique called serialization to pass objects. This technique allows the representation of an object (that is, its attributes and its methods) in the form of a character string that is directly interpretable by the receiver object.

8.4.1 Java RMI Architecture

The Java RMI allows communication between two Java entities located on two distinct Java virtual machines. The Java RMI implements the client–server model in which the client is either an applet or a Java application and the server is an object belonging to a Java application.

In order to access the object server, the Java client must obtain its address. It obtains this by asking for an entity which is called the Registry. The Registry acts as a name server. It has a table in which each object name is associated with its reference. Each reference contains the interface and the address of the object. It is important to observe that each object must have a unique name which distinguishes it from all other objects. By using the object reference, the client is then able to ask for the execution of a method on this object. This request crosses the following layers (see Fig 8.10):

- The stub/skeleton layer. The stub represents an image of the remote object. It possesses the same interface. Its function is to receive calls aimed at the remote object and to transmit them to the real object using the intermediary of the layer immediately below the remote object.

- The remote reference layer. This layer handles the semantic aspect of communication. It is in charge of the marshalling (ordering) function. It will also be in charge of the multi-cast function, that is, the ability to send the same request to all objects offering the same interface (this function will be implemented in the near future).

- The transport layer. This layer is responsible for the establishment of the connection as well as its management.

Every Java entity (application or applet) can use the Java RMI system. This contains the three layers described above, and runs on top of the Java virtual machine.

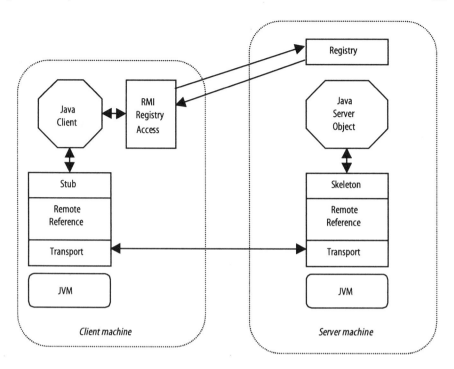

Fig 8.10 Architecture of the Java RMI system.

8.4.2 Stages in the Construction of Java Client and Server Objects

The construction of two Java entities of which one (the client) wants to send the request for execution of the methods on the other (the server) using the RMI mechanism, can be decomposed into four steps which are:

1. *Creation of the interface to the server.* In Java, the concept of interface is separate from the concept of object. It is desired to construct the interface which defines the methods that are accessible by the client. Only the names of methods and their parameters are defined. An interface contains no code. This interface must be accessible in a remote fashion, it inherits from the standard interface called *Remote* (see Fig 8.11).

2. *Creation of the server object.* The server object contains the code for methods described in the interface which it implements. This code will be executed when a remote request is transmitted across the RMI layers. From the Java code describing the interface and the object server, the bytecode for the server object is created by means of compilation (using the *javac* command).

3. *Creation of the Java client.* The Java client can be either an applet or an application. Let us consider the case of an applet. This is downloaded to the user machine using the Internet HTTP protocol. For reasons of protection, this applet can only communicate with objects found on the machine from where it originates. In order to communicate with one of these objects it must:

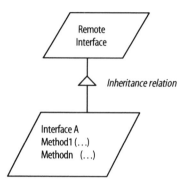

Fig 8.11 Interface A inherits properties from the standard interface Remote.

- generate a Registry request in order to obtain the reference to the desired object;

- execute the call to a method on the remote object. Note that at the level of Java code, the syntax for a call is the same as for one to a local object.

Contrary to the code in a CORBA object, the code for a Java client contains the call to the name server. The code for the client is thus "aware" of the fact that it calls a remote object. The applet is a Java package which includes the pre-defined classes: *java.rmi.*, java.rmi.registry.** and *java.applet.**.

4. *Creation of the server program.* At the server level, it is necessary to construct a Java application having as its role to:

- create the server object (this translates into the creation of an instance of the object server class);

- register this object with the name server (Registry);

- create and install a security manager in order to protect the server object against illegal access.

At this stage, the code for the client (applet) and the server exists. In order to visualize this, one can imagine that all the files containing the bytecodes of the different components are stored in the same directory. For example, if we refer to Figure 8.13, the directory is called *ClientServer* and contains:

- the bytecodes for the server object in file objectserver.class;

- the bytecodes for the client stub in file objectserver_stub.class;

- the bytecodes for the server skeleton in the file objectserver_skel.class;

- the bytecode for the client (applet) in file *Applet.class*.

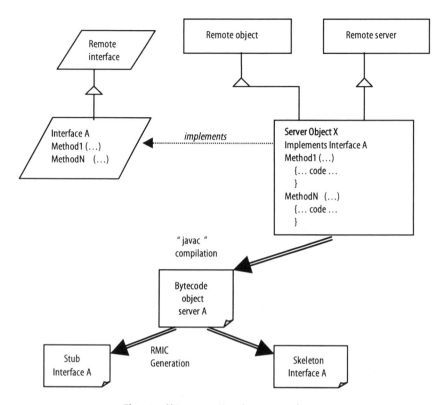

Fig 8.12 Object server X implements interface A.

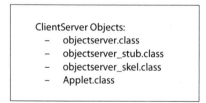

Fig 8.13 Set of files containing the code for the RMI protocol client and server.

8.4.3 Stages in the Execution of a Remote Method Invocation (RMI)

The stages in the performance of a client–server dialogue between Java objects using the Java RMI protocol are the following:

1. Start the name server. It is necessary to run the name server (Registry) on the server machine. It must be active.

2. Start the server object. It is necessary to start the server program so that the server object can run and that it is registered in the Registry.

3. Activation of the applet. An applet is always associated with a HTML page. This means that the user must download a HTML page referencing the file which contains the applet (for example, the *Applet.class* file in Fig 8.13). Typically, the latter is activated when it is downloaded or when the user redisplays the HTML page.

4. The applet generates a call to the name server (Registry) situated on the server machine in order to obtain the reference to the desired object.

5. The applet generates a call to a method on the remote object. This call is in fact locally redirected to the stub. The stub code no longer being loaded, the JVM class loader requests the downloading of the file containing this code (e.g., *objectserver_stub.class*).

6. When the stub is present, it transmits the request to the remote reference layer and waits for the reply.

7. Data belonging to the request are formatted (marshalling) and sent across the network with the server as their destination.[5]

8. On the server machine, the request is converted to the local format and the skeleton generates the processing request used for all local objects. The server object executes the method with the parameters which have been provided to it, then returns the result parameters to the skeleton. They are then returned to the client after having been converted to the standard format.

9. The remote reference layer for the client collects the parameters, converts them to local format and transfers them to the stub which returns them to the applet. This ends the call.

8.5 Java Beans and ActiveX

The expression "component-based software" is employed to describe a software model comprising an architecture and a set of application interfaces (APIs). This model allows the definition of components and their assembly when constructing applications. It has three principal elements, which are:

• Components. They are objects whose complexity varies from the simplest (e.g., push-buttons) to the most complex (e.g., spreadsheets).

• Containers. They are objects allowing the assembly of components. They offer an environment in which components can interact. Containers can also contain other containers and so on in a recursive fashion.

---

[5] The protocol that is currently used is JRMP which is not compatible with CORBA. Sun announced, in October 1997, that this protocol will be compatible with IIOP, the transmission protocol in CORBA.

- Scripts. They allow the initiation and direction of interactions between components. Scripts can be written in traditional languages such as C, C++ or Java or even in shell languages such as Tcl/Tk and JavaScript.

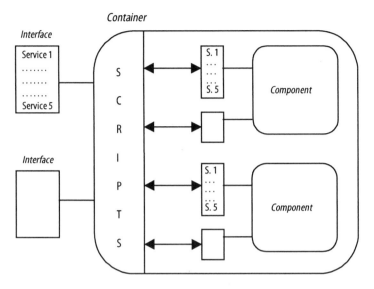

Fig 8.14 Theoretical model of software based on components.

In order to be usable, software based on components must offer a set of common services, which are:

1. Publication and discovery of the interface. When a component is put into a container, it must be able to identify itself and publish its interfaces. Thus, the other components learn of its existence and the way in which it can be communicated with.

2. Event management. In object technology, objects communicate by exchange of messages. An object generates an event (or a message) and the container is responsible for its delivery to its destination. Events can be generated by the user themselves (for example, by clicking on window) or by other objects (e.g., by modification of an object stored in a data base).

3. Persistence. Components must be able to store in a permanent (non-volatile) fashion certain information. This function of storage can be implemented in a very simple fashion using a sequential file.

4. Display control. There exist two types of control. The first type allows a component to control is appearance inside its own display space. The second type allows display control of a component inside a container. The programmer specifies the appearance of a component when it is constructed; however, the appearance can be modified by mechanisms that control the display of container.

5. Help in constructing applications. This service allows a component to expose its interfaces and attributes in order to be exploited by various tools. Relevant tools are, for example, for the editing, inspection and debugging in order to assemble components for the rapid construction of an application.

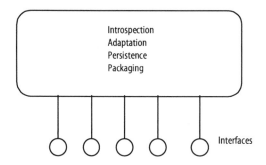

Fig 8.15 Characteristics of a Java Bean.

8.5.1 The Java Bean Concept

A Java Bean is a software component that is reusable and is written in Java; it is designed to be manipulated using graphical tools (e.g., Java Studio, Visual Age for Java, Visual Café, JBuilder, PowerJ, Java Workshop, etc.) A Java Bean contains Java classes and forms the basic elements for the construction of applets and/or Java applications. It can have multiple aspects: this can be a graphical component (e.g., push button, slider, graphical control, database display, etc.), or a non-graphical component containing a particular function (e.g., cost calculation, production optimization function, etc). A Java Bean has its own characteristics which are:

- Introspection. In order to be able to use a Bean, every tool that manipulates it must be able to analyze its structure. This is possible thanks to the function of introspection. This allows one to know the different methods available (their exact syntax) as well as the object attributes that the Bean contains.

- Customization. This function allows the Bean to be customized to the needs of the user (e.g., for graphical beans, it is possible to choose colours, size and character font, etc.)

- Persistence. This is possible thanks to the serialization function which allows the component to be encoded in a particularly compact format. This format also allows the transfer of an object across the network using RMI.

- Packaging. In order to be able to distribute Beans, they are stored as well as the tools necessary for their installation and execution in files with a particular format called *.JAR*.

The concept of a Java Bean was originally introduced by Sun in order to be used in the Internet context. Today, its use largely goes beyond this because it uses market standards. It is, for example, possible to construct distributed applications that are written entirely in Java, using CORBA object-based middleware.

8.5.2 ActiveX Components

The concept of software component is strongly linked to the concept of a composite document. A composite document is constructed by several applications in common, each being responsible for an element of the page of the document (e.g., text, table, graphic). In this model, the document serves as a container object. It offers an environment in which are defined the component interfaces (or applications) necessary for the construction of the page, as well as the means for communicating between these applications.

In the Microsoft model, the component is called an ActiveX. This name has evolved with its different versions: VBX for 16 bit Visual Basic components, OCX for 32 bit components, then finally ActiveX for distributed components. ActiveX components are compiled OLE objects (see Chapter 5) that conform to the COM model and to its extension to distributed environments (DCOM).

The natural evolution of the ActiveX component is to merge the concept of a composite document with the concept of a HTML Internet page. Thus, the construction of a HTML page can imply the downloading of one or more ActiveX components onto the user machine. To operate, each component must then register with the local OLE middleware. The browser then serves as the container inside of which the ActiveX components can execute.

8.5.3 Comparison between Java Beans and ActiveX

Java Beans and ActiveX are both software components. As such, they form the basic elements for the construction of distributed applications. Their comparison is interesting because they represent the two models that are currently the standard: the portable Java model, which is based on market standards, and the proprietary ActiveX model from Microsoft. Table 8.1 presents the main points of comparison.

The choice of an application construction model depends principally on the environment in which it must operate. When applications must be developed for a homogeneous Windows environment with a non-critical security level, the ActiveX model constitutes a very good choice. The ActiveX concept is well integrated with all Microsoft software and it is now usable for the construction of complex applications.

If one is undertaking the development of an Internet application, which requires a high level of security in a multi-platform environment, combining different types of network, the Java approach must be seriously considered. The current weaknesses of Java come from the lack of maturity of this technology, not to its basic principles. The Java language was introduced at the end of 1995. The road followed since then is impressive and there is no reason why it should stop. Maturity will come very quickly!

Table 8.1 Comparison of Java Beans and ActiveX

Java Beans	ActiveX
Uses standard CORBA object-based middleware.	Uses proprietary Microsoft middleware.
Are distributed as applets.	Form the element of distribution.
Are written in Java.	Are written in any language.
Are downloaded in the form of bytecodes that are executable on any platform.	Are downloaded in binary form, hence are executable only on a single platform (Intel/Windows).
When downloaded, an applet has a lifetime which is that of the associated HTML page.	When downloaded by Internet, they have a lifetime independent of the associated HTML page. They continue to live after it disappears.
Cannot use the resources of the machine onto which they have been downloaded (no access to local disk or to local operating system). This ensures that the downloaded code cannot destroy the environment on the receiving machine.	Can access all the resources of the machine on which they have been downloaded. This mechanism offers many possibilities for processing, but constitutes a weakness from the security viewpoint.
Have the support of many of the major actors in the market (Sun, IBM, Oracle, etc.).	Represents a proprietary technology owned by Microsoft.
Represents a technology in the course of definition and lacks maturity.	Forms a proven technology, well-integrated in the Windows environment.

9. *Introduction to Object Technology*

This chapter is a short introduction to the concepts of object technology. It only contains the material necessary for understanding the chapters dealing with the CORBA, OLE/COM technologies and with modelling. It does not pretend to be exhaustive.

9.1 The Concept of an Object

The concept of an object is, in fact, very familiar to us. Each day we use or we refer to objects. In our terminology, an object is identified by its *name* and is characterized by a set of *attributes* and *operations* that can be applied to it. Thus, an object can be a thing as real as a car or a cat. It can also be an intangible thing such as an idea.

In the example in Figure 9.1, the object car is referenced in a unique fashion by its registration number. Among its possible attributes, we can mention its colour and price; the actions (operations) which we can perform on it are, for example, driving it, buying it and perhaps wrecking it.

I. Jacobson[1] defines an object as follows: "An object is characterized by a number of operations and a state which records the effect of these operations." Under this definition, the state of an object is represented by the set of values of the attributes associated with it.

From the computing viewpoint, an object combines into a single entity the concepts of processing (operations) and data (attributes). Thus, when an industrial process is represented in the form of a collection of objects, the aspects of "processing" and "data" can be analyzed at the same time. This is in complete opposition to the traditional modelling approach which tries to separate the processing part from the data part.

---

[1] I. Jacobson, *Object-Oriented Software Engineering: A Use Case Driven Approach*, Addison-Wesley.

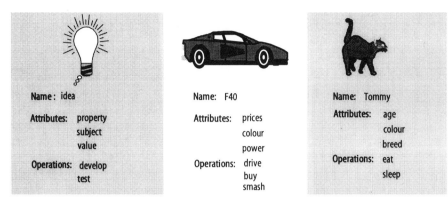

Name: idea

Attributes: property
                 subject
                 value

Operations: develop
                 test

Name: F40

Attributes: prices
                 colour
                 power

Operations: drive
                 buy
                 smash

Name: Tommy

Attributes: age
                 colour
                 breed

Operations: eat
                 sleep

Fig 9.1 An idea, a F40 and Tommy are each an object.

9.1.1 Concepts of Class and Instance

When a model is constructed from objects, it can be noted that some of the objects have common characteristics in terms of attributes and operations. It is then interesting to group the common properties into a single entity. Figure 9.2 shows an example in which the three objects – *Myrtle*, *Pushkin* and *Tommy* – identify three distinct cats, but which have common characteristics in terms of attributes and operations. Rather than individually representing each of them, we will use the concept of class to describe them.

A class contains all the attributes and operations common to the objects that it represents. The definition of a class given by Jacobson is the following:

> A class represents a mould for objects, describing their internal structure. The objects of the same class have the same definition for their operations and their attributes.

Following this definition, the class appears as an abstraction which describes the characteristics that are common to all the objects that are members of this class. In object technology, every object belongs to a class and is called an instance of this class. Jacobson defines an instance as follows:

> An instance is an object that is created from a class. The class describes the struc-ture of the instance (operations and attributes), while the current state of the instance is defined by the operations performed on that instance.

In the example shown in Figure 9.2, *Myrtle*, *Pushkin* and *Tommy* are instances of the class *Cat*.

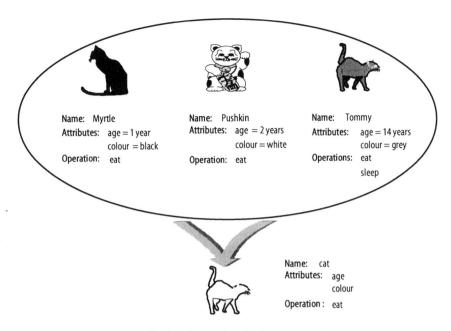

Fig 9.2 The class *Cat* describes what is common to all cats.

9.2 Principal Characteristics of Object Technology

9.2.1 Encapsulation

Encapsulation has, as its aim, the separation of the external aspects of an object (that is, those accessible by other objects), from the details of the implementation. What does this mean for the attributes comprising an object?

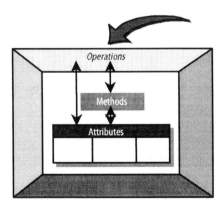

Fig 9.3 Encapsulation of an object.

9.2.1.1 Encapsulation and Operation

The operations associated with an object represent the actions that are possible and that can be requested by other objects. The external format of these operations must be completely defined. One possible syntax is the following:

operation_name([type parameter, parameter],[type parameter, parameter], ...)

The external format of an operation is called its *signature*. It is public. On the other hand, the associated piece of program (or code), called a method, is hidden. Thus, the user of an object knows how to call an operation associated with this object, but does not know how it is implemented.

9.2.1.2 Encapsulation and Attribute

The attributes of an object allow its state to be stored. The value of the attributes depend on the actions of the operations performed on that object. This means that they are not directly accessible to the external world. The only way to access them is to use a previously defined operation. By convention, the majority of languages have two standard operations to access those attributes one wants to be made public. In OMG[2] notation:

set_<attribute_name>(parameter)
get_<attribute_name>(parameter)

Example: The operation *set_colour(grey)* gives the value "grey" to the *Colour* attribute in the instance *Tommy* which belongs to class *Cat*.

From this fact, the name and type of each attribute are public, but the way in which each attribute is encoded is hidden.

The concept of encapsulation allows, by separating the exterior aspect of an object (called the *interface*) from its implementation, two objectives to be satisfied:

- offer, at the modelling level, the concept of object without having to worry about implementation details;

- offer, at the implementation level, the flexibility to choose the programming language in which to code the methods, and associate one or more appropriate methods with an operation.

9.2.2 Terminology and Representation

The development of software, no matter what technology is used, proceeds by phases, the principal ones being the analysis/design phase, the programming and the production phases. When the object approach is used, the perception of objects varies according to the phase in which one finds oneself. Thus:

---

[2] Object Management Group, International Standards Committee.

- In the analysis phase, one is only interested in the external aspect of the object – its name, its operations (with their signatures) and its attributes. The object interface is all-important. An object is then designated by the term *type*.

- In the programming phase, one is interested in the internal aspects of an object. It is necessary to program its methods, and to define the most appropriate way to represent its attributes. The term *class* is then preferred over object.

- In the production phase, when the application executes, object structures are created dynamically. These structures are called *instances*.

Figure 9.4 shows the three representations of the object concept.

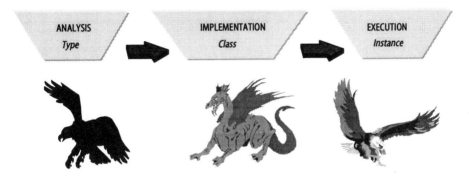

Fig 9.4 The three possible representations of an object.

In this book, we are mainly interested in the system modelling aspects, that is, with the analysis phase. In order to represent objects in our models, we will use Rumbaugh's notation.[3] Figure 9.5 shows the graphical notation used to represent an object in a model. Figure 9.6 shows an example of the representation of the object *Cat*.

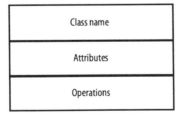

Fig 9.5 Representation of a type.

---

[3] J. Rumbaugh *et al.*, *Object-Oriented Modeling and Design*, Prentice Hall, 1991. Rumbaugh created the Object Modelling Technique (OMT) notation.

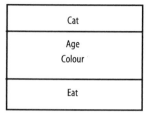

Fig 9.6 Example of a type.

9.2.3 Abstraction

When an object is structured, that is, when a representation is created such as that shown in Figure 9.6, the question arises as to its completeness. Must it identify and include all possible attributes and operations associated with an object? The reply is negative. To construct an object model means to construct an abstract representation of a material or immaterial entity. This abstraction must incorporate in the model those aspects of the object that are important in the context of the domain of concern, rather than try to represent the whole entity in all its aspects.

The domain in which the problem to be solved is to be found must be used as a discriminating factor. Thus, if the object car must be constructed, the attributes and operations chosen will be very different depending upon whether the software is for a salesman or a mechanic. Figure 9.7 makes this approach explicit.

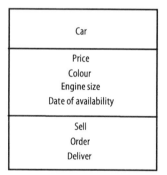 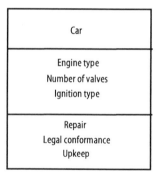

Fig 9.7 Two examples of abstraction of the *Car* object.

9.2.4 Static Relations

9.2.4.1 Inheritance

The construction of a model constitutes the analysis phase during which the objects being manipulated are called types. Early on, it is noted that certain types have common characteristics in terms of operations and attributes. For example, in Figure 9.8, the types *Salesman* and *Administrator* are very similar. These similarities can be extracted and grouped into a new type called *Employee*. A relation is therefore defined between this new type and existing types (*Salesman* and *Administrator*) called an inheritance relation. Using this relation, the *Salesman* and *Administrator* types inherit operations and attributes from the *Employee* type. This leads to the introduction, in each of the types *Salesman* and *Administrator*, of only those elements which serve to differentiate them. The common elements are collected in the *Employee* type. Figure 9.9 shows the final structure obtained using the Object Modelling Technique (OMT) notation to describe the inheritance link.

The concept of inheritance can be defined as follows:

> If a type X inherits from a type Y, the operations and attributes belonging to type Y also belong to type X. Type Y is often designated as the super-type and type X as the sub-type.

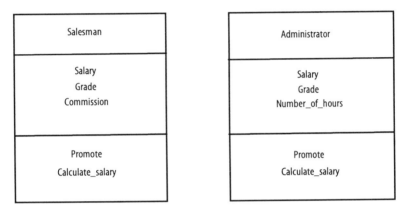

Fig 9.8 Types *Salesman* and *Administrator.*

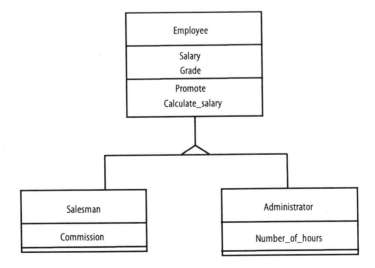

Fig 9.9 Inheritance relation between types.

The inheritance relation is sometimes called the generalization/specialization relation. If we consider this relation in the sense of sub-type to super-type, it can be seen that only the elements common to the sub-types are retained. It is a matter then of a generalization relation. On the other hand, if we consider this relation in the sense of super-type to sub-type, then elements are added in order to better characterize the sub-type. It is then a matter of a specialization relation.

The concept of inheritance leads to obtaining a model that is very concise. It contains only that which differentiates the types. Redundancy is thus avoided and information only exists in a single instance.

The inheritance mechanism allows a new type to assume previously defined attributes and operations. It is this which makes object technology encourage software reuse.

Another interesting property of inheritance is the way in which it facilitates updates. A modification at the level of the super-type is automatically carried over to its sub-types.

Abstract Types

An abstract type collects the characteristics in terms of the behaviour (operations) and state (attributes) of several sub-types so that these sub-types can inherit from it, and be specialized. An abstract type is differentiated from a concrete type by the fact that no instance can be directly obtained from it. The concept of an abstract type was introduced to ease the reuse of software and to optimize the overall model.

In the example shown in Figure 9.9, the type *Employee* is an abstract type. Therefore, no instance of it can be produced because instances have no sense. Only instances of the types *Salesman* and *Administrator* can exist. These two types are thus concrete.

9.2.4.2 Comparison between the Inheritance Relation and Instance Generation

The inheritance relation and generation of an instance are two very similar mechanisms which can easily be confused. A little clarification does not go amiss.

The inheritance relation exists between types or classes. It is, thus, used at the analysis and programming levels. Instance creation only exists when the application executes. It is only during the execution phase of the application that instances of a class can be created.

The inheritance relation is a static facility used at the model level. It can include abstract types. Instance creation is a dynamic mechanism that can be used only during the execution phase when instances are created from concrete types.

Figure 9.10 shows the distinction between these two mechanisms. Two instances are created, Terry and Stephen.

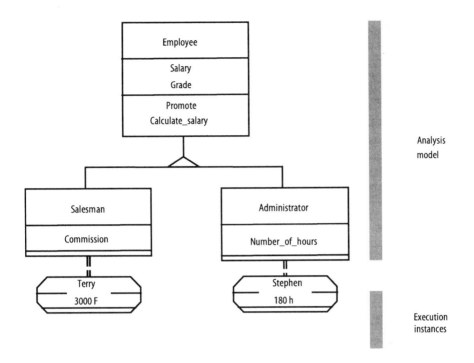

Fig 9.10 Inheritance relation and instance generation.

9.2.4.3 Overloading

The inheritance mechanism allows a sub-type to inherit attributes and operations from the super-type with which it is associated. It can, however, happen that the attribute and the operation that are inherited need to be redefined in the sub-type. The concept of overloading permits retaining the names of inherited attributes and operations while changing their definitions.

In the example shown in Figure 9.11, the abstract type *Employee* has the operation *Calculate_salary*. This operation is defined as returning the value of the *Salary* attribute. The inheritance mechanism transmits this operation to the two sub-types *Salesman* and *Administrator*. In reality, the calculation of the salary of an employee depends on their function. Thus, the salary of a salesman is defined as being equal to a fixed amount (represented by the attribute *Salary*) plus their commission (*Commission* attribute). The definition of the inherited operation *Calculate_salary* associated with the *Salesman* type is replaced by this new definition. This is the mechanism of overloading.

The calculation of the salary of an administrator is also different from that which is inherited from the *Employee* type. In the above example, it is equal to the sum of the *Salary* attribute plus the number of hours worked (represented by the *Number_of_hours* attribute) multiplied by the hourly rate. The substitution of this new definition for the one inherited forms an example of overloading.

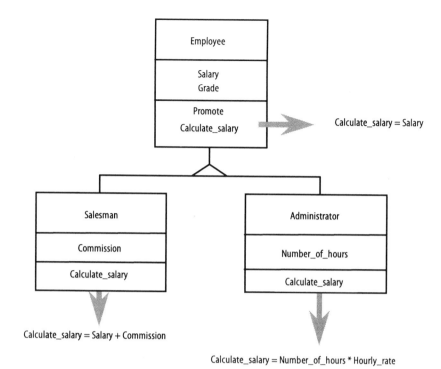

Fig 9.11 The overloading technique.

9.2.4.4 Polymorphism

The concept of overloading described above shows that an inherited operation can have a behaviour that depends upon the type in the hierarchy in which it occurs. This concept can be generalized to all types independent of inheritance relations. This is the technique of polymorphism which is defined as follows:

> We call polymorphism the capacity to allow certain types to react to the same operation in different ways, each according to its own fashion.

Some examples will make this principle more easily understood. In Figure 9.12 the operation *Talk* is applied to three different types (man, cow and donkey) with different results.

In information technology, to print a file is a very common operation. However, the operation performed differs according to whether the file type is "ASCII text" or "Postscript". Thus, the same operation name "print" corresponds to two behaviours, these behaviours being directly linked to the types to which they apply.

Another way of considering polymorphism is to say that the object type which sends a request does not have to know the type of the receiver. From this fact, the receiver type matters little provided that it offers the necessary operation. In this exchange, it is the receiver type which determines the interpretation of the operation to be performed.

Talk		Hello!
Talk		Moo
Talk		Hee-haw

Fig 9.12 Example of polymorphism.

The principle of polymorphism is very useful during the modelling phase of software development. At this level, designers are interested principally in the signatures of the operations and not by the description of their contents. Thus, in the above example about IT printers, the designer will have to identify the existence of the "print" operation on files of type "ANSI text" and "Postscript". It is not important for the designer to know whether or not these operations are different in terms of their implementation. What *is* important is the use of the most appropriate name for the operation to add to the model.

9.2.4.5 Aggregation

Aggregation characterizes a relation between types in which one type is composed of one or more other types. The component types are called parts and the composed type is called the whole. The whole represents the assembly of the parts.

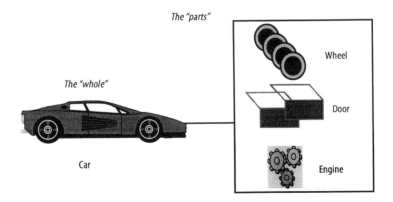

Fig 9.13 Example of the aggregation relation.

There exist several variants of this relation. They are:

- the relation "is composed of". In the example described in Figure 9.13, the *Car* type is composed of types *Wheel*, *Door* and *Engine*.

- The "containing–contained" relation. "An apartment contains a certain number of rooms". In this example, the *Apartment* type contains the type *Room*.

- The relation "belongs to". "Mr Davies is a member of the Automobile Club". In this example, the type *Automobile Club* forms the group to which *Mr Davies* belongs.

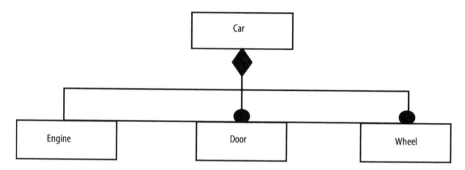

Fig 9.14 Example of representation of the aggregation relation in OMT.

Using the OMT notation recommended by Rumbaugh, the example of the relation depicted in Figure 9.13 takes the form shown indicated in Figure 9.14. In this notation, the symbol "◆" represents aggregation. The symbol "●" indicates that the type with which it is associated can exist in one or more examples. Thus, the last symbol shows that the *Car* type is composed of one or more doors and one or more wheels.

9.2.4.6 Comparison between Inheritance and Aggregation Relations

The inheritance and aggregation relations are static relations and object structures. The inheritance relation represents a state and thus can be explained using the verb "to be". This relation, as shown in Figure 9.15, is read as follows:

A Car is a Vehicle
A Truck is a Vehicle
A Van is a Vehicle

The aggregation relation describes possession and this fact is expressed using the auxiliary "to have". This relation, in the example shown in Figure 9.15, is read as follows:

A Vehicle has Wheels
A Vehicle has Doors
A Vehicle has an Engine

The combination of these two relations allows the very concise expression of complex structures. Thus, the example in Figure 9.15 expresses the fact that the types *Car*, *Truck* and *Van* all have *Wheels*, *Doors* and an *Engine*.

In the inheritance relation, represented by the "▲" symbol in Figure 9.15, every modification to the super-type necessarily implies a modification to the associated sub-types. The same does not hold for the aggregation relation in which the modification of a part has no impact on the whole. Thus the inheritance relation allows automatic broadcasting of modification while the aggregation relation limits all modifications to an object to itself. This difference in operation between these two relations is fundamental and divides experts in object technology into two camps. Some of them think that it is necessary to use the inheritance mechanism and have incorporated it into the CORBA object model. Others, conversely, think that it is dangerous because it is difficult to control and prefer to use the aggregation relation. This is the choice that Microsoft made in its OLE/COM object model.

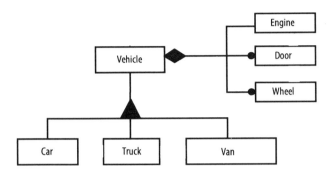

Fig 9.15 Inheritance and aggregation relations.

9.2.5 Links and Associations

Besides the structural relations that can exist between objects (inheritance and aggregation), there exist relations expressing the interaction between objects and objects. A link represents a physical or conceptual relation between two instances of objects. For example, *Peter works for the Post Office*.

A link is an instance of an association. The concept of association is used at the modelling level while that of link exists at the level of an object instance. Thus "a person *works for* a company" forms the association relative to the link *works for* between the instances Peter and Post Office.

An association represents an active form and it is often labelled by a verb. In OMT notation, the association "a person *works for* a company" is represented as shown in Figure 9.16.

Each association has a cardinality. In the example in Figure 9.16, the cardinality is defined as varying from zero to *n*. This means that a company can have from zero to *n* employees. However, the concept allows one to be very precise in explicitly describing the number of instances desired. In the above example, a company employing a maximum of 20 persons will have an association whose cardinality will vary between 0 and 20.

An association does not necessarily generate links. In this case, it serves only to provide information to the model's reader.

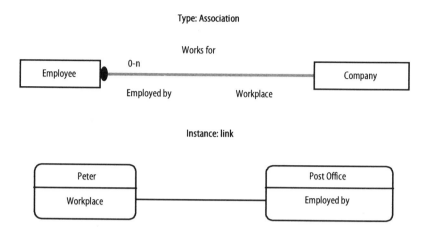

Fig 9.16 Example representation of an association in OMT notation.

If links are generated, the *roles* of each association become instance attributes. A role is a label attached to each end of the association; it indicates the function played by the associated type when viewed from the perspective of the other type. In the example in Figure 9.16, the company plays the role of the workplace for the employee in the association *works for*. If a link is created, each instance of the *Employee* type will have an attribute *PlaceOfWork*.

Reciprocally, *employed by* is the role played by the set of employees of the company in the association *works for*.

9.2.5.1 Many-to-Many Relations

In order to describe the real world, it is sometimes necessary to be able to characterize a relation between two types using attributes which are appropriate to this relation. This is particularly the case in many-to-many relations. The example in Figure 9.17 describes not only the fact that a company can have several employees, but also an employee can work for several companies. It is desirable to be able to describe the qualification of each employee for the post they occupy. Because the relation between the two types *Employee* and *Company* is complex, it must be described using attributes. The notation proposed by Rumbaugh is that used in Figure 9.17.

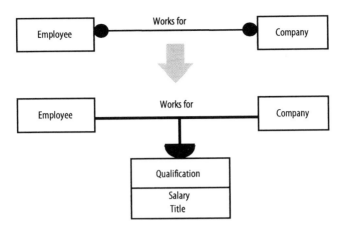

Fig 9.17 Example representation of a many-to-many association in OMT notation.

10. MethodF™: A Method for Object-oriented Analysis and Design

MethodF[1] facilitates the integration of new applications with existing ones in order to respond to the information processing needs of companies. This method allows the translation of these needs into an infrastructure in which applications, old and new, can easily be inserted. The emphasis is on the reuse of existing software at the programming and design levels.

The aim of MethodF is the realization of an implementation model that integrates old and new applications.

10.1 Introduction

MethodF comes from two methods – Ivar Jacobson's Object-Oriented Software Engineering (OOSE) and the Object Modelling Technique (OMT) of James Rumbaugh (Fig 10.1).

OOSE is characterized by the analysis technique called *Use Case* which allows the fine description of business processes, beginning with the identification of their fundamental component objects. This technique also allows the formalization of the system interface to be modelled. The description of the Use Case finally serves as a script for testing the resulting product.

OMT is a very well-known and highly popular method for analysis and design. It is used by the majority of object modelling tools. The OMT notation offers an efficient and concise way to represent the different types of object used by MethodF.

The characteristics of MethodF make it a unique method because:

---

[1] MethodF is a registered trademark of Digital Equipment Corporation. For a complete description of MethodF, the reader should refer to the document "Framework Based Environment: MethodF," September 1995, order no. AA-QC50B-TH, Digital Equipment Corporation.

- it is oriented towards the integration of existing applications while other analysis methods are concerned with the development of new applications;

- it allows reuse at the level of the analysis/design model which contrasts with the methods which encourage reuse at the code level;

- it offers tools allowing the specification of adapters for the easy integration of existing applications.

MethodF is much in line with the theme of this book, for it is concerned with the construction of information systems that are composed of distributed objects and based on applications that have already been written.

The goals of MethodF are:

- to analyze the business independent of the applications which are or will be used to automate some parts of it;

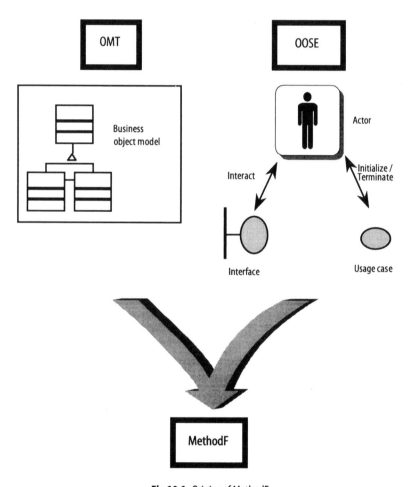

Fig 10.1 Origins of MethodF.

- to model the business in a logical fashion and then to establish the correspondence with existing or new applications;

- to construct a model of the business which is at the same time independent of processes and business applications;

- to encourage the architect to reuse existing models.

MethodF like every software development methodology consists of four main phases which are:

1. The *specification* phase. The aim of this phase is to delimit the system to be constructed, to identify its users and to create the specification of the system in a particular form called a *scenario*.

2. The *analysis* phase. This phase assembles the needs which the solution must satisfy. These needs must be expressed in business terms.

3. The *design* phase. This phase starts with the detailed specification of the interfaces of the objects as they will be incorporated in the final system. The analysis model is modified in order to incorporate existing objects in the reference models or in models that have already been constructed.

4. The *implementation* phase. This phase details the way in which the methods associated with the operations are implemented. Either this is a matter of existing applications which must, thus, be "dressed up" in order to present the desired interface, or it is a matter of new applications which must then be developed. This phase also starts the description of the physical distribution of software components on the various machines that are available.

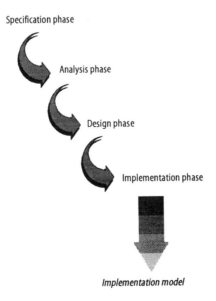

Fig 10.2 Phases of MethodF.

10.2   Specification Phase

The goal of the specification phase can be divided into three parts:

- define the objectives of the system to be constructed;
- identify the users;
- write the specification.

MethodF insists on the importance of the client and assigns them a central role in all phases of the project. The client is the person for whom the software is constructed; the software must satisfy all requirements as far as processing is concerned. That is why the client must belong to the team defining the specification of the final system.

10.2.1   Objectives of the System to Be Constructed

The definition of the objectives of the system to be constructed leads to the identification of its limits, its users and its principal functions.

Definition of its limits leads to optimization between the two following extremes:

- carry out the project in a highly limited domain in order to increase its chances of success and do this in a reasonable time;
- carry out the project on a large scale and with high complexity.

The evaluation of the extent of the domain to be covered by a project has, as its aim, the definition of the optimal domain size. When a problem is encountered that is too large to be handled effectively, a well-known technique for solving problems can be employed; this technique consists of breaking the problem down into a set of smaller sub-problems which can be analysed separately (divide and conquer). This technique applied to the management of a project was formalized in a method called RAMS (Requirements Analysis for Management Systems).

The use of the RAMS method allows the identification of the client's primary business activities as well as the flow of information between them. The matrix representation is a valuable aid in helping the client describe their business, the users, of each sub-system and the data flows.

The matrix's diagonal (see Fig 10.3) contains all the sub-systems comprising the domain being studied. A sub-system is either an organization that is external to the company, or an internal department, or a function, or an application. The matrix that is obtained is square; that is, it contains as many rows as columns. The flow of information is described by inserting a data description into a cell of the matrix such that:

- this cell is either on the same row as the source sub-system (or emitter sub-system), or
- this cell is in the same column as the destination sub-system (or receiving sub-system).

This approach is clearly recursive, that is, it can be applied again to each subsystem in the initial matrix.

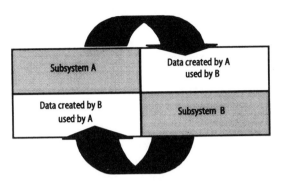

Fig 10.3 The matrix associated with the RAMS method.

When the RAMS matrix is finished, each component of the system under study is identified and its limits found. It is then simple to choose the domain for study.

In the example shown in Figure 10.4, the system being considered allows the salesman direct access to information about the products that are available in a product catalogue. It allows the input of orders and the organization of production. The cells forming the diagonal of the matrix contain the different functions. The information flow between the functional modules is described in the cells that do not fall along the diagonal.

Initial project study area

Catalogue search	List of products to be ordered			
Product characteristics	Order input	Client order		
	Order status	Order decomposition		Manufacturing orders
Catalogue		List of components	Product management	
	Date of dispatch			Planning

Fig 10.4 Example of a RAMS matrix.[2]

---

[2] "Framework Based Environment: MethodF," September 1995, order no. AA-QC50B-TH, Digital Equipment Corporation.

10.2.2 Actor Diagram

After having defined the limits of the system, it is important to identify who its users are. Here, the word actor will be preferred to the word user. An actor can be a person or another information system. People interact with the system typically via a graphical interface. Systems interact via the intermediary of software interfaces (API: Application Programming Interface). Let us note that an actor is not simply a person (in the case of a human) who uses the system, but a person playing a certain role with respect to the system. Thus, a person can play several roles with respect to any given system.

The use of the RAMS matrix forms a good way to present the actors of a system. The information flow described in this matrix shows the communicating entities. Thus, in Figure 10.4, if we consider the *Accept Order* sub-system, it can be observed that three actors are associated with the action: *Look in Catalogue, Decomposition of Order* and *Planning*. On the other hand, the *Accept Order* sub-system is itself an actor with reference to the *Decomposition of Order* sub-system.

Each actor, according to the role it plays, uses the system in a different way. Each role represents a Use Case which is described in the form of a scenario. The scenario defines the interaction between the actor and the system in detail, and consequently allows the precise definition of its interface and therefore its limits.

In order to represent the different actors in the system under consideration, the actor diagram is constructed. If the reader refers to the system described in Figure 10.5, it will be seen that the actor diagram for the *Accept Order* sub-system has been drawn, and it will be observed that there are three actors (*Look in Catalogue, Decompose Order* and *Planning*). The client is not a direct actor since they interact with the *Look in Catalogue* sub-system. In order to gain clarity, they can always be included in the final diagram.

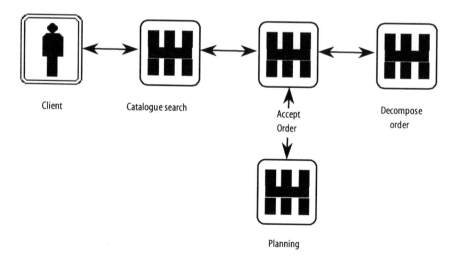

Fig 10.5 Example of an actor diagram.

10.2.3 Specification: Use Case

The operation of a system can be described in many ways. We will be interested here in the one which yields the actor's viewpoint. An actor plays one or more roles with respect to the system and each role represents a use case described by the scenario. Thus, a scenario represents the interaction between the actor and the system as well as the operation of the resulting system. A scenario makes precise by its detail each action and each behaviour. It also specifies the temporal order in which the different actions are performed.

The set of use cases, each written in the form of a scenario, can also serve as a specification for acceptance tests on the final system.

The notion of a use case was introduced by I. Jacobson who defined it as follows:

> A use case is a particular way of using the system by using only some of its functions. Each use case comprises a complex sequence of events which are initiated by an actor and specify the interactions between this actor and the system. A use case is therefore a particular sequence of operations, realized by the actor and the system in the course of their dialogue. The set of use cases covers all the different ways of using the system.

An important aspect of use cases is that they describe what happens at the system interface level. It is concerned with *what*, that is, in what the system does and what the user sees. It is not interested in *how*. This approach is consistent with the philosophy of object analysis which invites the observation of the exterior aspects of things before becoming concerned about the way in which they can be efficiently implemented.

The complete description of the operation of a system implies that several scenarios must be available. These, inevitably, cover common domains. In order to express the relations that exist between several scenarios, a graphical notation was introduced. Each use case is represented by an oval and two types of links exist between two ovals: they are the addition link and the optional addition link (see the example in Fig 10.6).

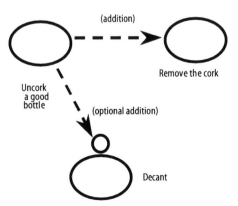

Fig 10.6 Example of use case combinations.

10.2.3.1 Description of a Use Case

The description of a use case consists of the sections shown in Figure 10.7.

- Title
- Summary
- Actor(s)
- Pre-conditions
- Scenario
- Exceptions
- Post-conditions

Fig 10.7 Sections comprising the description of a use case.

10.2.3.2 Example Use Case

Title

Request information about products.

Summary

A salesman consults a catalogue using a set of search criteria. The catalogue selects the products which meet the criteria.

Actor

A salesman.

Preconditions

The product line is known to the salesman.

The search criteria are known.

All the products satisfy at least one selection criterion.

The catalogue is open and ready to accept queries.

Scenario

The scenario describes the list of transactions performed in the course of the use case. It is recommended that each phrase is numbered in order to find it more easily if the need occurs. If it is necessary to refer to another use case during the description, it can be written between square brackets.

1. A salesman consults the catalogue in order to obtain the list of all the product lines.

2. The catalogue returns the list of all the product lines.

3. The salesman chooses a product line.

4. The salesman queries the list of characteristics associated with the selected product line as well as the list of all the products that it contains.

5. The product line returns the characteristics as well as the list of products belonging to this line.

6. The characteristics of the product line are displayed as well as the list of products in the chosen product line that are being sold.

7. The salesman chooses a characteristic of the product line.

8. The salesman requests the list of the products that satisfy the chosen criteria in the chosen product line. [Exception: no products found].

9. The product line returns the products satisfying the given criteria (criterion).

10. The products satisfying the criteria (criterion) are (is) displayed.

11. Repeat steps 5 to 8 zero or more times.

12. The salesman chooses a product.

13. The salesman requests the price and quantity in stock of the chosen product.

14. The system returns the price and quantity in stock of the product.

15. The catalogue displays the price of the product and the number in stock.

Exception

No product found. This appears when the combination of search criteria eliminates all the products belonging to a given product line. The salesman is warned that no product satisfies their request. If no other combination of criteria returns at least one product, the use case terminates.

Post-conditions

The salesman uses the price and the number of items in stock of the chosen product(s).

10.2.4 Summary

Specification phase

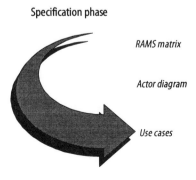

RAMS matrix

Actor diagram

Use cases

Fig 10.8 MethodF: specification phase.

10.3   Analysis Phase

The analysis phase has three aims:

- Construct the object-based analysis model which describes the interfaces of the component types for the final system.

- Construct the dynamic models which will allow the validation of the static model and make the dialogue between the user interface and the system more precise.

- Construct the interface model which associates types with existing applications.

10.3.1   The Object-based Analysis Model

Each use case is analyzed in order to construct a *viewpoint* on the objects which participate in the transactions described in the scenario. Each viewpoint on the system shows the existence of interfaces through which the identified objects are "seen". Only the attributes and the operations of these objects which are necessary to the transactions appear. This allows us to model only those elements that are indispensable to the final system. The union of all viewpoints forms the Object-based Analysis Model.

In each viewpoint, two categories of type can appear. They are:

- the interface object (or interface) type;

- the analysis object (or analysis) type.

10.3.1.1   The Interface Object Type

An interface object represents the medium connecting an actor and some analysis types. This medium receives requests from the actor which it transfers to the analysis types and returns the replies. In a symmetrical fashion, the requests can be initiated by the analysis objects in order to be transmitted to the actor.

The identification of interface objects is simple since it ensures communication between an actor and the system. From this, there exists at least one per actor. However, an actor can play several roles, each role can require an interface object.

Interface Object

Fig 10.9 Representation of an interface object.

The term "interface object" is used in order to differentiate it from the very general concept of interface to the object theory. The interface object is situated at the frontier between the system and the external world. It can be implemented either by a graphical interface in the case where the actor is a human, or in the form of data structures in the case where the actor is another system.

An interface object has neither attributes nor operations. It can make requests to any analysis object. Figure 10.9 shows how an interface object is represented. The interaction between an interface object and an analysis object is indicated by an arrow whose head shows the sense of the request (see Fig 10.10).

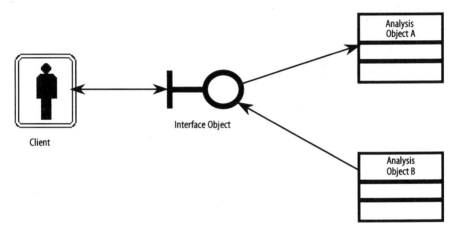

Fig 10.10 Interface object and its interaction with analysis objects.

10.3.1.2 Analysis Type

An analysis type represents a specification of a business object and, as such, possesses attributes and operations. The analysis types are identified from scenarios associated with use cases. They appear in the models corresponding to viewpoints as well as in the analysis object model. Analysis types are represented graphically as shown in Figure 10.11. Analysis types allow the formalization of data and their behaviour.[3]

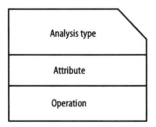

Fig 10.11 Representation of an analysis type.

---

[3] Analysis types are equivalent to the entity types in Jacobson's OOSE method.

10.3.1.3   Links Used in an Analysis Model

Three types of link are used in order to specify communication or architectural relations in the analysis model. They are:

- The *architecture* link. This term covers the relations of generalization, aggregation and association. These connections exist between analysis types but not between interface types.

- The *interactive* link. This link indicates that an entity (interface or analysis type) can make a request to another entity. This link, whether uni- or bidirectional, is written as an arrow indicating the sense of the interaction (from the sender to the receiver).

- The links *referenced by* and *obtained by*. These are two examples of the interactive link and both use an interface object. The "referenced by" link shows the interaction between an interface and an analysis type. It denotes that the interface type can request the execution of operations by the analysis type. This connection is represented by an arrow directed from the interface type and pointing towards the analysis type. The "obtained by" link associates an analysis type with an automated interface type (an automated interface type represents available application software). This link indicates that the operations of the analysis type are implemented by the software represented by the automated interface type. It is represented by an arrow pointing from the analysis type towards the interface type.

10.3.1.4   Stages of Construction of the Analysis Model

The following actions must be performed in order to construct the analysis model:

- identify the analysis types and their attributes;
- construct a data dictionary;
- identify the associations between different types;
- identify the operations associated with the different types;
- organize and simplify using the inheritance link;
- repeat the above steps as many times as necessary.

Identification of Analysis Types

Analysis types are identified from the scenarios associated with the use cases. The majority of these types are easily found for they correspond to everyday concepts. However, other types can be more difficult to find when it is a matter of, for example, concepts (update, trajectory, etc.).

On the other hand, it is also very easy to identify more of them than necessary. The difficulty is only to list those which are really indispensable. This implies that one should work in a structured fashion. The first step consists of making a syntactic analysis of the text. This analysis reveals the types, their attributes, their operations, and the relations that obtain between them.

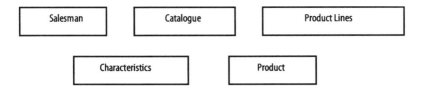

Fig 10.12 Entities extracted from the scenario connected to the request for information about products.

The (very) general principles for syntactic analysis are the following:

- Every noun (or naming) appearing in the text is either an object or an object's attribute.

- Verbs represent operations on objects.

These two principles need (clearly) to be applied. The first difficulty is to decide whether an entity is an attribute or an object. Two decision criteria can be useful:

- When an attribute has itself got attributes, it constitutes an object. This object will be related to the object to whose description it makes a contribution via an association link.

- The mode of use. If an entity is used independently of other entities, it must form an object. If, on the other hand, it is tightly associated with another entity and never used in isolation, then it constitutes an attribute of this entity.

At this stage, we can be content with identifying objects without relating them to each other. Thus, in the scenario described in section 10.2.3.2 above, the first five lines allow, *a priori*, the identification of the types listed in Figure 10.12.

It can be noted that the *Salesman* entity is in fact an actor in the system and must not therefore figure in the model. On the other hand, *Characteristics* is tightly connected to the *Product Line* entity. This leads to the intermediate model shown in Figure 10.13.

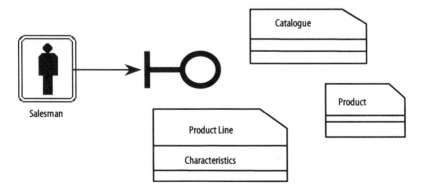

Fig 10.13 Intermediate model.

Construct a Data Dictionary

In order to avoid all confusion, it is necessary to carefully define the terms that are used. In particular, synonymous terms should be noted. This must be done for object names, attributes and operations as well as for associations.

Identify the Associations between Different Types

The associations between objects are often described in the scenario by verbs. They correspond to actions performed by one object on another. Associations also include physical connections (beside, part of, contained in), possession (of, element of), or relation (is married to, manages, works for).

There exist two other ways to identify relations between objects:

- when an object needs to access another object an associative connection between the two objects must exist;

- when one object communicates with another, it must be able to answer the following question: how does object X know the address of object Y with which it wants to communicate? The answer to this question is detailed in section 10.3.2.3 below.

The relationships identified in section 10.2.3.2 above are depicted in Figure 10.14.

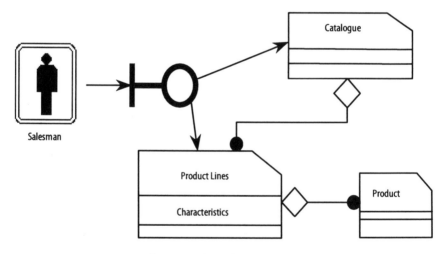

Fig 10.14 Relations between types.

Identification of Operations

There exist three principal types of operation. Each is described by the verb acting on the object. These three types are:

- read or write some information (a piece of information is represented by an attribute);

- create or destroy an object;

- operations which affect the behaviour of the object.

The operations identified in part of the scenario in section 10.2.3.2 are shown in Figure 10.15.

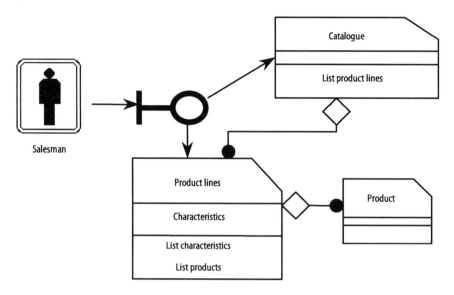

Fig 10.15 Identification of operations.

10.3.2 Dynamic Models

Every aspect of the system related to the concept of time and to the changes it induces are described in dynamic models. The development of dynamic models allows the capture of the execution flow of the system and forms an excellent means to validate the static model.

Two dynamic models are used in MethodF, they are event diagrams and state transition diagrams.

10.3.2.1 Event Diagram

The event diagram used in MethodF is akin to the *interaction diagram* proposed by Jacobson.[4]

This diagram represents the execution flow of the system such as it is described by a given use case. Therefore, with each use case, there is an associated diagram which describes the interaction between objects in the analysis model.

A particular formalism was introduced to construct event diagrams. This formalism must not, however, hide the primary aim which is to describe the system's execution flow in a detailed fashion.

---

[4] I. Jacobson, *Object-Oriented Software Engineering*, Addison-Wesley, 1992.

Objects interact via the intermediary of events. Each event corresponds to the request by an object for the execution of an operation on another object.

In the chosen representation (Fig 10.16), objects are represented by a vertical bar, in some order, the aim being the clarity of the diagram. The interface object is represented by a multiple line. The time axis is vertical; time runs from top to bottom. Comments (expressed in free-form text or in the form of pseudo-code) are set to the left of the hatched property. The event is described by a horizontal arrow going from the sending object towards the receiving one. The operation associated with the receiving object whose execution is requested by the event is represented by a rectangle superimposed on the line denoting the object.

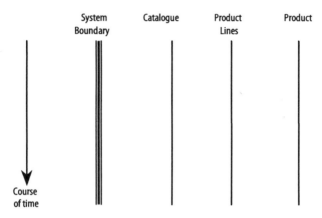

Fig 10.16 Structure of an event diagram.

Figure 10.17 shows an extract from the event diagram associated with the scenario for the request of information about products.

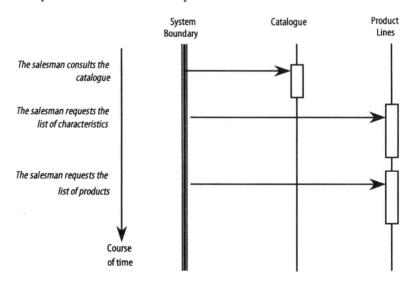

Fig 10.17 Partial event diagram relative to the scenario in section 10.2.3.2.

It is very important for each event to provide the list of input and output parameters in order to verify that the interface to the objects is well defined and that the model can operate. An event must not be seen as a simple procedure call. Different types of event exist. They are:

- Synchronous call. The client object makes a request and waits indefinitely for the reply. This is similar to a procedure call.

- Synchronous call with timeouts. This call is synchronous; it waits for a specified time for the reply. If no reply arrives in the specified time, the client takes up its execution again.

- Uni-directional call. The client sends a request and does not wait for a reply. Here, the request only contains input parameters.

- Asynchronous call. The client sends a request but continues its execution without waiting for the reply. It will be notified by the communication system if a reply arrives.

- Deferred synchronous call. The client sends a request but continues its execution without waiting for the reply. The client will not be notified of the arrival of the reply and must interrogate the communication system to discover if one exists.

- Persistent call. A client sends a request which remains active until a server object is able to process it. The duration of the life of the request can exceed that of the client. From this, the client must not wait for a reply.

- Broadcast. Two modes exist. The first mode consists of sending the request to a determinate number of objects. The second consists of sending the request to a well-known place where interested objects are registered in order to receive requests.

10.3.2.2   State Transition Diagrams

The state transition diagram shows the different states which can be found in an object, as well as the events causing the state changes. These diagrams allow the enrichment and validation of the analysis model. They describe the conditions under which an operation can be performed on an object. The analysis model used does not provide any information of this kind. It confines itself to describing interface objects.

The concept used in Figure 10.18 indicates that *object A* can be in *state1* and that under condition *c1*, event *E1* will allow it to pass to *state2*.

State transition diagrams allow the description of object behaviour in greater detail. Let us recall that this is not the aim of MethodF which is interested mainly in interface objects. For a more detailed study of these state transition diagrams, the reader should consult Jacobson's book.

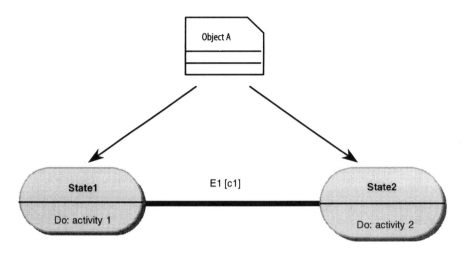

Fig 10.18 Notation used in the state transition diagrams.

A state can itself have sub-states. In the notation being used, sub-states are depicted inside their super-state. Thus, in Figure 10.19, the *Motor* object has two states, *Stopped* and *Running*. The *Running* state has two sub-states: *Started* and *Turning*.

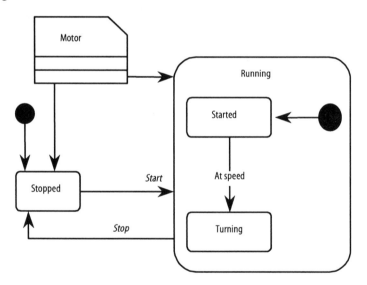

Fig 10.19 State transition diagram. Example of states and sub-states.

10.3.2.3 Static and Dynamic Links

At this stage, it is useful to consider the different types of links that appear in static and dynamic models.

Static Model

This model contains passive structural links. Some of these links will reveal themselves at the implementation level as pointers. They then express the fact that one object knows the address of another.

Dynamic Model

This model contains action links. An action link between an object *A* and an object *B* signifies that object A requests an operation in object B to be executed. This implies that object *A* knows the address of *B*. To achieve this, several methods can be employed.

- A structural link exists between two objects which need to communicate. This connection is expressed in the static model. It will be implemented in the form of an attribute associated with the object *A* containing a pointer to object *B*.

- The address of the target object (e.g., *B*) comes to the sender object (e.g., *A*) in the form of a parameter connected with the execution of an operation. This must then be very clearly indicated in the static model.

- The target object is a "public" object, that is, it is known throughout the system. This implies that a naming function be available in the execution environment.

MethodF recommends therefore that a *naming diagram* be used; this allows the representation of types from which public instances are generated. This naming diagram is distinct from the object analysis model. It contains the object type and a public instance to which it is attached by a dashed arrow; the type *Name* and instance *Object_Name* to which it is attached by a dashed arrow. Finally, an arrow connecting the instance of the name to the instance of the public object is annotated with the name of the public object. Figure 10.20 presents an example of this representation.

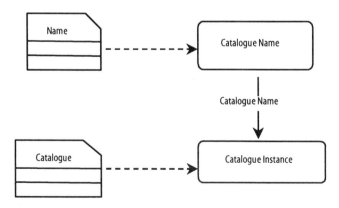

Fig 10.20 Example of the naming of a public object.

The target object belongs to a particular class of object with which it will be very hard to associate a name. In this case, all of these objects must be grouped into another object which forms the object group, which will be a public object. For example, the *Client* objects can be grouped into an object *Client_DataBase*.

The construction of the dynamic model allows the validation of the static model and shows up inter-object reference problems. If no static link exists between two objects that are likely to communicate, the designer must ensure that the sending object has a way to obtain a reference to the receiving object (see above).

10.3.3 Interface Model

The analysis object model has as its goal the identification of the components of a system independently of the way in which they are used. Each component (or object) is described in isolation without including information about its use context.

MethodF is based on the hypothesis that the implementation of a business process, whether manual or automated as software, must be able to be modifiable while the interface of the components (objects) remains the same. The heart of the activity in the approach suggested by MethodF is concentrated on the definition of these interfaces.

MethodF encourages reuse of existing software and the aim of its analysis phase is to ensure that for each type (object) that is identified, there exists one or more available applications that can automate its behaviour. If this were not the case, the specification for the development of a new application would have to be provided in the phase following design. In order to establish the connection between the analysis model and existing software, the interface model is used.

In the interface model there are two types of actor: the *human* and the *automated* actor. The human actor is familiar to us. Its connections with the system are of type "reference", that is, the actor can request the execution for an operation of an object that belongs to the system. In a symmetrical fashion, the system can ask the human actor to provide it with some data. The automated actor allows the existence of a piece of application software to be represented. A "provided by" link between an analysis type belonging to the system and an automated actor means that the operations of the analysis type are implemented by the software represented by this actor.

In the interface model, every interaction between the system and the actor brings in the interface object. This is shown in Figure 10.21.

The steps allowing the construction of the interface diagram are the following:

- create a new diagram containing all the types in the analysis model as well as all identified interface objects;

- introduce the human actors identified in the actor diagram and connect them to the corresponding interfaces;

- for each available application, introduce an automated actor as well as an interface object and connect these entities together;

- run over each type in the analysis model and try to connect it with one or more interface objects linked to an automated actor using a "provided by" link. If, for a given type, no link is possible, this means that there exists no application available to implement its function. A new application will have to be implemented.

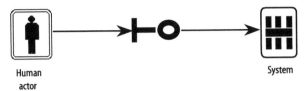

Interaction between a human actor and the system.

Interaction between the system and an automated actor.

Fig 10.21 Representation of the two types of interface object.

At this stage, all the information is available to pass to the design phase and to the business object model. Figure 10.22 provides an example of an interface model.

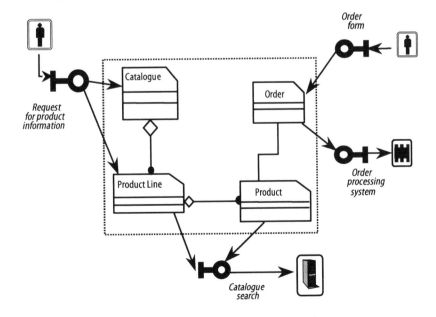

Fig 10.22 Example of an interface model.

The analysis model can contain a large number of types, and this leads to representing the interface model as shown in Figure 10.23.

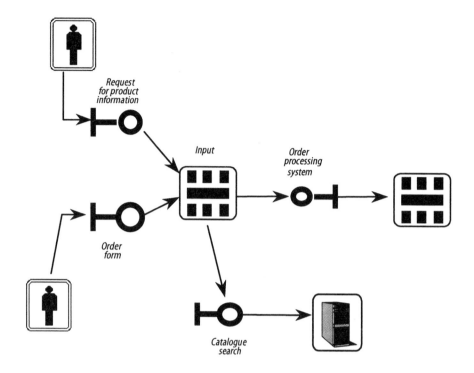

Fig 10.23 Example showing interfaces related to the Order Input system.

10.3.4 Summary

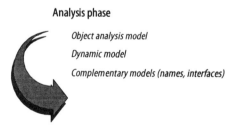

Fig 10.24 MethodF: analysis phase.

10.4   Design Phase

The point of entry to the design phase consists of the object analysis model which describes the characteristics of the components of the system to be implemented. The aim of the design phase is to develop the business object model from which is produced the IDL code describing the interfaces of the various objects.[5] In this phase, there comes the implementation of the models that were previously constructed.

The construction of the business object model is performed in several stages:

- Design of object types. This aim is achieved either by the reuse of types that are already available in the model library, or by creating new types.

- Location of objects. To ensure that references to instances of defined types are available to their users.

- Generation of objects. A generator object must correspond to the objects that are dynamically generated.

- Detail the interface of each object type in order to generate the IDL code.

10.4.1   Design of Object Types

The business object model contains object types, in contradistinction with the analysis model which contains analysis types. The design phase consists of constructing object types from analysis types.

10.4.1.1   Object Type

Object types represent analysis types that are completely specified. This means that a detailed description of their interface in the Interface Definition Language can be deduced from them. Remember that the aim of MethodF is to encourage the reuse of objects at the design level. This is why a certain number of basic objects and domain objects were defined. This assumes that a software analysis and design tool is used in order to construct and store these objects in its database. It is in this database that we can go digging in order to reuse its contents.[6] The representation of an object type is shown in Figure 10.25.

In the approach described here, the assumption is made that we have available a library of object models which are either basic models[7] or models relating to a type

---

[5] There are several versions of this language. Here, we will be concered with the one that allows us to describe the interface of the objects using the CORBA standard.

[6] Tools examples are ObjectPlus from the Palladium company and ROSE from Relational. A certain number of object models exist and are available through this tool.

[7] Note that such models exist in industry. Digital Equipment uses a methodology whose modelling tool contains a set of basic models and a set of models pertaining to various industries.

of industry (domain models) or, finally, models developed in the course of previous projects. The question of the design of each object type associated with the analysis types must be raised. Four possibilities exist:

- create a new object type;
- design the object type using inheritance based on existing types;
- design the object type using delegation;
- create a data structure.

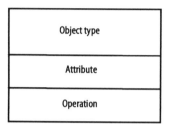

Fig 10.25 Representation of an object type.

10.4.1.2   Creation of New Object Types

If, after consultation of the different object models available, it seems that no object or combination of objects corresponds to the type to be designed, it is necessary to create a new object. At this stage, the process of creation of a new object is very simple. It consists of introducing an object having the same name, the same attributes and the same operations as its associated analysis type into the business model diagram. These attributes and operations must be detailed. This object is connected to the other objects by the same connections as those described in the analysis model.

10.4.1.3   Design by Inheritance

Design by inheritance is possible when the analysis type possesses attributes and operations which are semantically identical to those of the object(s) that appear(s) in the models being used.

In this case, the existing object is introduced into the model under construction as well as the object associated with the type being considered and these two objects are connected by an inheritance link. It is then necessary to remove the object associated with the inherited attributes and the operations. We only keep the attributes and operations needed by the associated operation in the pre-existent object.

In this process, it is highly probable that the names of attributes and/or operations associated with the existing object and with the analysis type will not correspond even though they are semantically equivalent. Rather than change them in the analysis model, it is advised to note in the data dictionary that the two terms are synonymous.

Example of Design by Inheritance

In this example (Fig 10.26), the object type associated with the analysis type *Order* is designed by inheritance from the two existing objects *Order* and *CustomerOrder*.

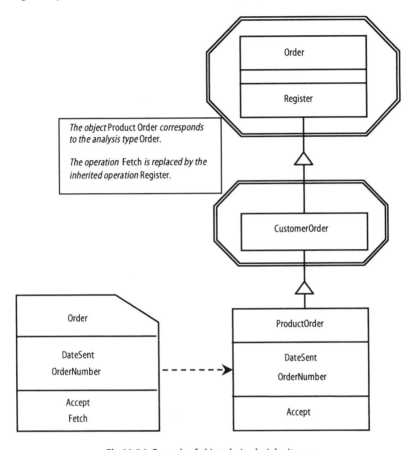

Fig 10.26 Example of object design by inheritance.

In the analysis that has been done, the *Order* type has two characteristics in common with the pre-existing *Order* object. Thus the operation *Fetch* is equivalent to the *Register* operation on the existing object. On the other hand, the attributes *DateSent* and *OrderNumber* which appear in the analysis do not appear in the *Order* object. In order to be able to reuse the existing models, the following actions must be taken:

- Make an object whose name must be changed in order to avoid the existence of two objects with the same name correspond to the analysis object *Order* (new name: *ProductOrder* for the object).

- The new object *ProductOrder* has two attributes, *DateSent* and *OrderNumber*, as well as the *Accept* operation.

- Incorporate into the model being constructed the pre-existing objects *Order* and *CustomerOrder* then establish an inheritance link with the *ProductOrder* object.

- Observe that the terms *Fetch* and *Register* are synonyms and that the term *Register* is used in the object model and belongs to the *Order* object.

This approach allows the reuse of a model and thus of the code associated with it (in this example, the *Fetch* function is already available). Figure 10.26 shows the final object model corresponding to this example (in this figure, the pre-existing objects are inside double lines indicating the model from which they come).

10.4.1.4 Design by Delegation

When an analysis type has operations which appear in an existing object type, and when this analysis type can be considered as a set of the pre-existent object, then design by delegation can be used. It then allows the addition of an operation in the object description by indicating that it belongs, in fact, to another object.

The process of creating an object type by delegation goes as follows:

1. Introduce the analysis type into the business object model.

2. Introduce the pre-existing object type.

3. Create an aggregation link between these two types.

4. Draw a propagation link (an arrow pointing from the analysis type towards the existing object) and label this connection with the name of the delegated operation.

5. Transform the analysis type into an object type.

Figure 10.27 shows an example of design by delegation in which the analysis type *CorporateSales* has an operation *CalculateTotalSales*. This operation is already defined in the existing object type *CountrySales*. The *CorporateSales* type can appear as being the set of *CountrySales* objects. On the other hand, the *CalculateTotalSales* operation is the same as that defined at the country or corporate levels. It thus appears in the description of the objects *CorporateSales* and *CountrySales*, and the fact that it is identical in all these cases is specified by the propagation link indicating that it is delegated to the level of the *CountrySales* object. Consequently, there is only a single instance of this operation.

10.4.1.5 Creation of a Data Structure

During the design phase, it is necessary to decide whether an analysis type becomes an object, or if it is preferable to design it as a data structure. This decision is strongly connected to the "size" which influences the flexibility of the final system as well as its performance. In some object-oriented languages, every entity is an object. This is the case, for example, in the Smalltalk programming language in which even an integer is an object. In our approach, objects can be distributed, and therefore a certain "size" is necessary in order to optimize the traffic across the network.

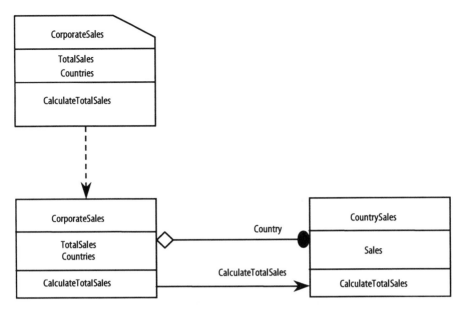

Fig 10.27 Example of design by delegation.

When a type is represented by a data structure, it is necessary to decide where the associated operations are located. The traditional approach leads to the introduction of the concept of a container object which can be characterized as follows:

- a container object contains multiple instances of the same data structure;

- data structures do not possess object references and cannot thus execute operations;

- data structures must possess an access key;

- a container object has operations which act on its content at the individual and collective levels.

In the example shown in Figure 10.15, where several analysis types are depicted, if we assume that the *Product* type is implemented in the form of a data structure, then the type *ProductLine* becomes a container object. The object model associated with this analysis model is shown in Figure 10.28. It will be noticed that a data structure in the model is represented by a simple block under which appears the label <structure>. The container object is identified by the fact that it has an aggregation link to the structures and operations belonging to these objects.

10.4.2 Location of Objects

This work has already been performed during the analysis step but becomes again necessary for the added object types. The procedure is the same as that written in section 10.3.2.3.

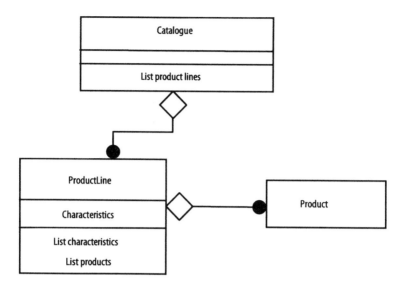

Fig 10.28 Example of the structure of data in an object model.

10.4.3 Object Generator

Because object instances do not arise from spontaneous generation, it is necessary to ensure that for every type which produces instances, there is an associated object generator.

An object generator is an object which creates instances of other objects. This implies that it has a creation operation for a given type.

The process of defining a generator object is the following:

1. Define the creation operation for instances and associate it with the generator object.

2. Draw an instantiation connection between the generator object and the model object.

3. Label this connection with the name of the operation which creates instances.

Figure 10.29 gives an example of the representation of a generator object. It will be observed that the information appearing in the object model has no effect on the IDL code that is generated. It only allows, and this is already a great deal, the assurance that the generation of instances is foreseen in the model.

10.4.4 The Business Object Model

When all the steps described above have been performed, the object model is finished. At this stage, its description must allow the direct generation of IDL code.

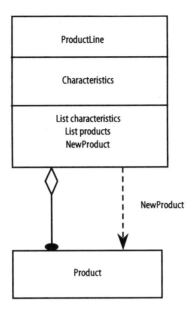

Fig 10.29 *ProductLine* is the instance generator for *Product*.

This assumes that each operation is completely described: the type of its arguments and whether they are input or output or input–output parameters.

The object model completely describes the interface of all the objects appearing in the system. It remains to find out how these objects are implemented. This is the goal of the Implementation phase.

10.4.5 Summary

Design phase

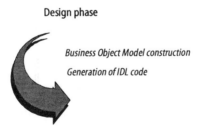

Fig 10.30 MethodF: design phase.

10.5 Implementation Phase

The aim of the implementation phase is to construct the implementation model which describes the physical solution. This objective is achieved when the correspondences between objects in the business object model and the existing applications are established.

At this stage, it is useful to define some terms. Thus,

- An object type possesses attributes and operations. The physical implementation of an attribute is a piece of data. The physical implementation of an operation is a method.

- Adapter. In the final physical system, existing applications are interconnected by adapters to the infrastructure bus. An adapter is a sequence of code whose interface represents one or more methods, and whose code translates this interface into comprehensible requests for the existing application(s) in order to execute the method or methods.

10.5.1 Types Used in the Implementation Model

Three types appear in the implementation model:

- the implementation type;
- the group type;
- the adapter type.

10.5.1.1 Implementation Type

The implementation type constitutes the implementation of an object type. It is graphically represented as in Figure 10.31. Just like object types, it has attributes (data) and operations (methods).

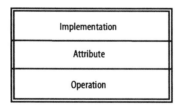

Fig 10.31 Representation of an implementation type.

10.5.1.2 Group Type

The group type allows the collection of several implementation types in order to implement a single object type. This case appears when the implementation types are distributed across several adapters. The group type is graphically represented as in Figure 10.32. In order to indicate that an implementation type belongs to a group type, an aggregation link is used. In the example in Figure 10.32, the implementations *Page1* and *Page2* belong to the type *Book*.

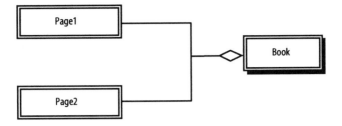

Fig 10.32 Representation of a group type.

10.5.1.3   Adapter Type

An adapter represents a sequence of code allowing the connection of one or more applications to the infrastructure. From this, an adapter contains implementation types. The graphical representation of an adapter is given in Figure 10.33.

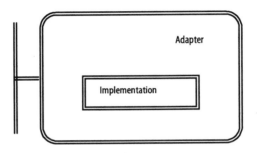

Fig 10.33 Adapter and association relation.

10.5.2   Associations Used in the Implementation Model

Three types of associations appear in the implementation model:

- residence association;
- implementation association;
- reference association.

10.5.2.1   Residence Association

This relation implies that the code (represented by an implementation type) which executes the operations and which contains the data structures representing the attributes of an object type must appear in the adapter. The adapter here plays the role of a server.

At this stage, implementation constraints must be taken into account. Thus the object model describes an inheritance mechanism between interface objects. This must be translated at the implementation level. However, the programming language that is used is not necessarily object-oriented. It is, in fact, typically quite the opposite. This implies that the implementation of an object must offer not just its own operations and its attributes, but also all of those inherited from parent objects. This operation is called "flattening the inheritance hierarchy". This association relation is shown in Figure 10.33.

10.5.2.2 Implementation Association

The correspondence between an object type and an implementation type is expressed by the implementation link. This link indicates that the implementation implements that which is described by the object type. Because of inheritance, the implementation must also implement the interfaces of the parent objects (Fig 10.34).

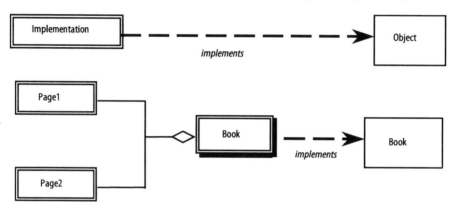

Fig 10.34 Representation of the implementation link for an object type.

Since the object model also contains interface objects, it is necessary to be able to make them correspond to an implementation. This implementation is necessarily an adapter type and it is understood that it fulfils all the functions associated with the interface type. The implementation link also allows the specification of this correspondence.

Fig 10.35 Implementation link for an interface object.

10.5.2.3 Reference Association

When an adapter makes requests to instances of an object type, it then behaves like a client to this type. This relation is expressed as a reference link between the adapter and the object type (see Fig 10.36).

Fig 10.36 Reference association.

10.5.3 Implementation Considerations

10.5.3.1 Shared Instances

When an object is implemented using several applications containing the data structures and methods of this object, and when these implementations are distributed across several adapters, we then speak of distributed instances. In Figure 10.37, the *Employee* object has two attributes, *age* and *profession*, as well as two operations, *pay* and *promote*. The implementation of this object requires two applications A and B, implementation A offering the attribute *age* and the operation *pay*, and implementation B offering the attribute *profession* and the *promote* operation.

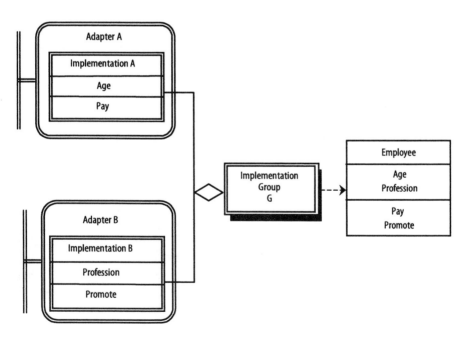

Fig 10.37 Example of shared instances.

10.5.3.2   Example of the Implementation Model

Let us consider a company employing mechanics whose salaries and employee numbers are recorded in the *Personnel* application. On the other hand, there exists the *Equipment Maintenance* application which contains information on the current task and the level of expertise, and also on the salaries and employee numbers of the workers. In this application the employee numbers are more detailed. It is desired to implement the pay and promotion of an employee using a *Processing Flow* system. The implementation model describing this example appears in Figure 10.38.

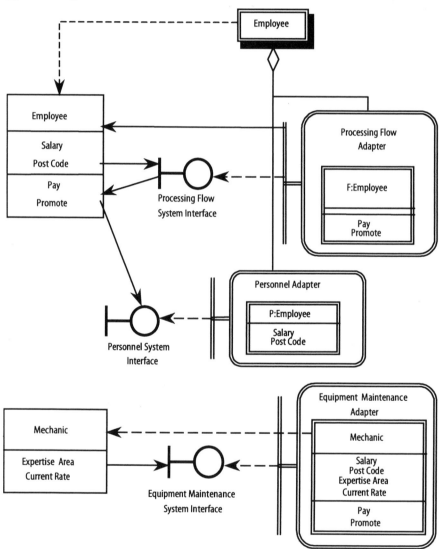

Fig 10.38 Example of the implementation model.

In this same figure, it can be seen that the *Employee* object has two links of type "produced by": one with the *Processing Flow* system, the other with *Personnel*. This tells us only that the interface to the *Employee* object is implemented using these two systems and without giving us any more details.

The "implements" link between the *Personnel System* and the *Personnel* adapter indicates that this interface is implemented by this adapter.

The reference link between the Processing Flow adapter and the *Employee* object indicates that Processing Flow is a client of Employee and will make requests of its instances.

The implementation P:Employee resides in the *Personnel* adapter. The implementation F:Employee belongs to the *Processing Flow* adapter. A group of implementations (Employee) resembles these two implementations (aggregation link). An implementation link connects this group to the *Employee* object. Thus, the interface to the Employee object is completely realized by these two implementations. The two attributes *salary* and *employee number* exist in the *Personnel* application and the two operations *pay* and *promote* are implemented in the *Processing Flow* implementation.

10.6   Summary of MethodF's Principal Steps

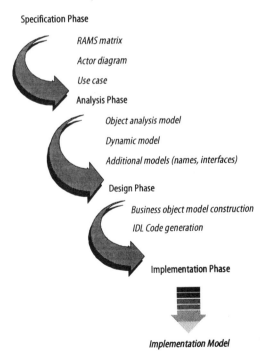

Fig 10.39 MethodF: the main development phases.

11. Conclusion

The different middleware technologies studied in this book allow inter- and intra-application inter-operability. Typically, for a given application composed of distributed elements, the RPC and ORB technologies are used. When there are several existing applications which must co-operate, the technologies of message queue, transaction monitor or ORB are used. A company can have a specific strategy for a critical application, and in parallel develop a strategy for their range of software in order to ensure coherence in the processing of data in a heterogeneous environment.

The middleware described in this book concerns applications which are referred to as being *mission-critical*, that is, those which are essential to the performance of the activities of a company. These applications are to be distinguished from decision-support software. The latter use a form of middleware which is referred to as direct access to data (DAD), such as SQL Gateways, ODBC, or EDA/SQL. These kinds of middleware, appealing as they are at first sight, have considerable weaknesses at the level of data integrity. Their use is not recommended for critical applications, the study of these kinds of middleware was deliberately omitted from this book.

This book rests on the basic assumption according to which the needs of companies will be best satisfied by a separation of functions rather than by a separation of data, such as that provided by DAD middleware. The separation of functions made possible by RPC, message queue or ORB technologies, is perhaps more difficult to program but offers better reuse of software components and is of higher performance.

Middleware based on the separation of functions evolves towards the concept of an object-oriented interface. This does not mean that the distributed components are necessarily objects but can be traditional encapsulated software which offers an object-based interface. These kinds of middleware are intended for critical applications, and the latter often requires the concept of transaction. Thus the evolution of middleware can be seen as follows:

- It will offer the functions of transaction monitors with dynamic invocation of object-oriented interfaces. Such middleware will allow, in addition to the exchange of messages, handling of servers and restarts from failures.

- RPC and message queue technologies will become the supporting technologies used by middleware of the object-oriented transaction monitor type.

11.1 Choosing Middleware

The choice of the middleware most appropriate to the needs of a company is difficult for several reasons:

- Middleware represents the infrastructure of all the information systems in the company. It is a matter, therefore, of a medium-term choice involving the future of the company. In this context, it is imperative to buy middleware from companies whose continued existence for the medium-term cannot be doubted.

- The technology is still being developed. Some years are still required before it achieves a decent level of maturity. From this viewpoint, 1998 seems to be a key date. If a choice must be made before this date, it must assume a rapid return on investment and leave open the possibility of replacing the software in some years' time. However, the future costs can be reduced if it is assumed that:

  o the approach is based on the concept of a high-level interface;

  o the concept of a service is associated with each interface;

  o the middleware product that is selected conforms to a standard or is offered by a manufacturer capable of supporting evolution of their products.

The immaturity of the market for middleware products must not, however, act as a break on the use of these technologies which can offer an undeniable advantage to the successful running of a company. Let us recall that middleware can be used inside a distributed application (e.g., a tool akin to Forté[1]) or in a set of applications. Table 11.1 suggests several criteria which help when choosing a middleware technology or product.

Table 11.1 Criteria for middleware selection.

Criterion	Message queue	RPC	ORB	Transaction monitor	Specific products
Transaction concept	No	No	No	Yes	Forté
Based on standards	No	Yes	Yes	No	
Synchronous/ Asynchronous	Async.	Sync.	Sync.	Async.	
Inter-application	Yes	No	Yes	Yes	
Intra-application	No	Yes	Yes	No	Forté
Integration of existing applications	Yes	No	Yes	Yes	
Good expertise in object technology in business			Necessary		Forté

---

[1] Forté is the name of a piece of software for the construction of object-oriented distributed applications. The middleware of this tool is proprietary, but is open towards the middleware presented in this book, that is RPC, message queue and CORBA technologies.

There are always many risks in predicting the future, but we can reasonably think, given current moves, that:

- The three-tier client–server model will be implemented using a graphical client based on Internet technology. This means that the user interface will be written in HTML and that the communications protocol will be HTTP or IIOP. The two other stages of the application will be executed on machines situated inside the company.

- RPC technology will be relegated to second place. However, the services offered by the DCE environment will be used by the highest level protocols.

- Asynchronous communication still has a long life before it, because it allows the user to work in an off-line fashion. This is perfectly suited to the case of the mobile worker.

- Object-based middleware will need a long time to become current.

11.2 The Complete Approach: From Company Requirements to Middleware Infrastructure

The study of middleware would be totally incomplete if it were limited to the technologies alone. The technologies are only valuable if they can be related to problems whose solutions they allow. The link between the needs of a company and middleware is possible, and this tenfold increase in interest in these technologies. Because their architectural possibilities are directly subjected to the needs of the company, they offer the flexibility which is indispensable to the satisfaction of these needs. This connection is realizable thanks to two things:

1. The concept of an interface which characterizes each component connected to the middleware bus. This concept allows the description of the set of services offered by the infrastructure.

2. The object-oriented methodology which allows the construction of a model for the interfaces which is sufficient to meet the users' needs. By doing this, this methodology contributes to the reduction of the complexity associated with the design and with the processing of distributed systems.

Figure 11.1 summarizes the entire approach. The interfaces are represented in the form of electric plugs and outlets. The middleware bus in the form of a large cable connects them. The design methodology consists, from the specifications provided by the user, to the construction of an object model. In this model, the external aspect of every object forms an interface. This is generated automatically in an appropriate programming language so that it can be implemented. On the other hand, the information available at the modelling level is exploited in order to permit the processing of the resulting distributed system.

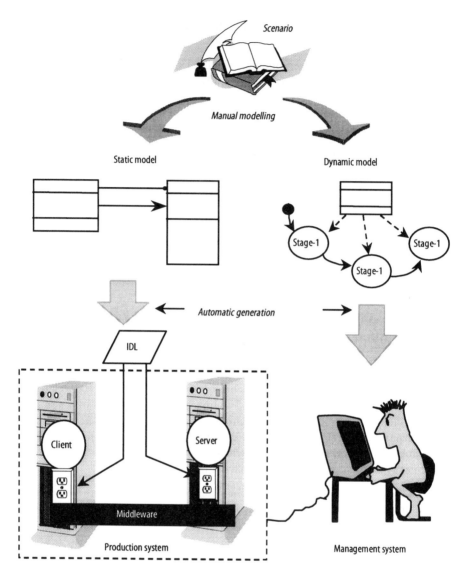

Fig 11.1 Global approach to designing, constructing and managing a distributed system.

Bibliography/Cybography*

Acly, E. *Middleware: 1996 Worldwide Markets and Trends*, International Data Corporation, Framingham, MA.

Boar, B. *Implementing Client/Server Computing*, McGraw-Hill.

Brockschmidt, K. *Inside OLE2*, Microsoft Press.

Colonna-Romano, J. and Srite, P., *The Middleware Source Book*, Digital Press.

DECmessageQ documentation: http://www.digital.com/info/decmessageq.

Digital Equipment Corporation (1995) *Framework Based Environment: MethodF*, Order No. AA-QC50B-TH.

Digital Equipment Corporation, *Object-Broker: Overview and Glossary*, Order No. AA-Q9KJA-TK.

Dilley, J., *OODCE: A C++ Framework for the OSF Distributed Computing Environment*, Hewlett-Packard. Email: jad@nsa.hp.com.

Falguière, C. (1996) *Internet and Distributed Applications: Describe Sounded Architectures to Build Applications over the Internet*, Digital Equipment Corporation, Sophia-Antipolis, France.

Fowler, M. (1992) *A Comparison of Object-Oriented Analysis and Design Methods*, OOPSLA '92.

Ghernahouti-Hélie, S. (ed.) (1994) *Client/Serveur, Les outils du traitement réparti coopératif*, Masson.

Jacobsen, I., (1992) *Object-Oriented Software Engineering: A Use Case Driven Approach*, Addison-Wesley.

Kirkley, J.R. and Nichols, W.G. (1995) "Integrating Applications with Digital's Framework-based Environment", *Digital Technical Journal*, Vol. 7, No. 2.

Laverdure, L. (1993) *NAS Architecture Reference Manual: Middleware for Building Distributed Applications*, Digital Press.

MIA Joint Research Project (1991) *Multivendor Integration Architecture, Technical Requirements*, Nippon Telegraph and Telephon Corporation.

---

* This term does not appear in the dictionary yet; it denotes references to documents available over the Internet. It was suggested to me by Jean-Claude Grattarola, Maître de Conférence at the University of Nice-Sophia-Antipolis.

MOMA, the standards: http://www.moma-inc.org/home.html.

Mühlhäuser, M. *et al.* (1993) "DOCASE: A Methodic Approach to Distributed Programming", *Communications of the ACM*, Vol. 36, No. 9.

OMG: general information. http://www.omg.org/.

Open Software Foundation, *Introduction to OSF DCE*, Prentice-Hall.

Orfali, R. *Client/Server Programming with CORBA Objects.*

Orfali, R., Harley, D. and Edwards, J. *Essential Client/Server Survival Guide*, Van Nostrand Reinhold.

Ovum Ltd (1996) *Ovum Evaluates: Middleware*, Ovum Ltd, 1 Mortimer Street, London W1N 7RH.

ProtoSoft Inc., *Object Plus, Reference Manual*, ProtoSoft Inc., 17629 El Camino Real No. 202, Houston, TX 77058.

Renaud, P. *Introduction to Client/Server Systems*, Wiley.

Rumbaugh, J. *et al.*, (1991) *Object-Oriented Modeling and Design*, Prentice-Hall.

Rye, J. (1996) *Applying OMG's CORBA and Microsoft's OLE in a Distributed Heterogeneous Object Environment*, DECUS US, June.

Serain, D. (1995) *Client/Server: Why? What? How?*, International Seminar on Client/Server Computing, IEE, IBM La Hulpe, Belgium, October.

Siegel, J. and Frantz, D. (1996) *CORBA Fundamentals and Programming*, Wiley.

Soley R. (ed.) (1992) *Object Management Architecture Guide*, Object Management Group.

Soley, R. (ed.) (1993) *Common Object Request Broker: Architecture and Specification*, Object Management Group.

Glossary

ActiveX	The Microsoft software component. It is a compiled OLE object which is fully DCOM compliant.
Applet	A piece of Java code which can be downloaded on any client machine.
AltaVista	Generic name for a family of Internet products from Digital Equipment Corporation.
API	Application Programming Interface.
CDS	Cell Directory Service.
CGI	Common Gateway Interface.
COM	Component Object Model.
CORBA	Common Object Request Architecture.
DCOM	Distributed Component Object Model.
DDE	Dynamic Data Exchange.
DFS	Distributed File System.
DLL	Dynamic Link Libraries.
DNS	Domain Name Service.
DSOM	Distribued System Object Model.
DTP	Distributed Transaction Processing.
Encapsulation	Technique employed in object technology allowing the separation of the external aspect of an object (interface) from the details of its implementation.
GDS	Global Directory Service.
GIOP/IIOP	General Inter-ORB Protocol/Internet Inter-ORB Protocol.
HTML	HyperText Markup Language.
HTTP	HyperText Transfer Protocol.
Hypertext	Name given to a document whose text contains references to other documents.
IDL	Interface Definition Language. This language allows the definition of the interface to servers. There are several versions of this language: OSF/DCE RPC IDL is the standard language for RPC technology; OMG

207

	IDL is the standard language for object-based CORBA middleware; MIDL is the Microsoft language for defining interfaces to COM objects.
IIOP	Internet Inter-ORB Protocol. IIOP is a network communications protocol recommended by the CORBA 2.0 standard.
Interface	Describes the list of services that a server can offer. An interface is described in a specific language called IDL.
Intranet	Network within a company constructed using Internet technologies.
Java	Programming language introduced by Sun Microsystems expecially designed for Internet.
Java Bean	This is a Java software component designed for reusability.
Java RMI	Java Remote Method Invocation. This is the Java middleware which is based on IIOP.
JVM	Java Virtual Machine. Set of programs residing on the client machien to execute applications.
Kerberos	Security utility allowing user authentication. Kerberos was developed by Massachussetts Institute of Technology.
LAN	Local Area Network.
LFS	Local File System. This service is a part of the OSF/DCE environment.
MethodF	Complete method for the development of object-oriented software. This method was defined by Digital Equipment Corporation.
Middleware	American word created to denote a layer of software for the exchange of messages.
MOM	Message-Oriented Middleware.
NetworkOLE	Object-based middleware from Microsoft. NetworkOLE is a registered trademark of Microsoft.
Object	Entity denoted by a unique name, whose state is characterized by attributes and whose behaviour is defined by operations.
ODBC	Open Database Connectivity. ODBC is a Microsoft product.
OLE	Object Linking and Embedding. OLE is the name of a technology created by Microsoft.
OMG	Object Management Group. International group responsible for the definition of standards for object-based middleware. In 1996, more than 700 companies were members of this organization.
OMT	Object Modelling Technique. This method was created by Rumbaugh.
OOSE	Object-Oriented Software Engineering. Development method for software defined by Jacobson.
ORB	Object Request Broker. Component of the CORBA object-based middleware allowing request handling.
OSF/DCE	Open Software Foundation/Distributed Computing Environment.

Platform	This term, in this book, denotes a computer and its operating system. Thus, a machine with an Intel processor using the Windows-NT operating system is a platform that is different from a machine using the same operating system but with an Alpha processor.
PostScript	Standard language used to describe documents to be printed.
Procedure	Programming entity collecting a set of instructions that perform a determinate function. The name and the parameters of a procedure constitute its signature.
RAMS	Requirements Analysis for Management Systems.
RPC	Remote Procedure Call.
Server	In the client–server communications model, the server is the entity which offers services.
Skeleton	In CORBA terminology, the server stub is called the skeleton.
SOM	System Object Model (from IBM).
Stub	A stub is a sequence of code generated automatically and which allows the connection of client and server to middleware.
TCP/IP	Transmission Control Protocol/ Internet Protocol. The Internet network is based on TCP/IP.
Thread	Execution path of a program.
URL	Uniform Resource Locator. This represents the standard way of designating a resource (e.g., a file) on the Internet.
UTC	Universal Time Coordinated. This service is part of the OSF/DCE environment.
Uuid	Universal unique identifier. This number is generated in such a way as to be unique in space and time.
WAN	Wide Area Network.
Wrapping	Software tools exist allowing the rapid enveloping of an application. Jabberwocky is one of these tools.
World Wide Web	Set of data of every type (text, audio, video, etc.) available on the Internet.

Index

abstract type 156
abstraction of object 154
ACID properties 20, 78
ACMSxp 22-3
ActiveX 144, 147
   Java Beans compared 147-8
actor diagram 170
adapters 194
   object 73-75
   server 73
adapter type 194-5
AddRef function 85-7, 92
address, physical 5, 52
address space 89-91, 98
   disjoint 90
   single 89
administration machine 56-7
agent 64-5, 78
   structure of interface 75
aggregate 61
aggregation mechanism 92, 100, 159
Alpha 22
analysis object 174-5
analysis model *see* object-based analysis
   model
analysis phase, MethodF 173-86
analysis type 174-6, 187-90
API *see* application programming interface
applets 127, 132-3, 135-44
   execution of 137
application code 11, 14
application objects 66
application programming interface (API)
   87, 123, 144, 170
application services 66
applications
   availability of 3
   code 11, 14
   integration of 2, 4
   old 2, 125
architecture link, analysis model 176
ASCII 11, 38, 51
association 161, 195
asynchronous call 181

asynchronous communication 9, 33-5, 37,
   64, 72
atomicity of transactions 20
attribute-value pairs 115, 117
attributes, object 17, 149
   encapsulation and 152
authentication 60
authorization 60
automation technology 95

basic object adapter 73, 75
Bento container objects 102
big-endian 51-2
binary level, standard at 82, 84
broadcast call 181
broker 64, 75
browser 24-6, 108, 110
bus, communications 1, 4, 9, 15, 203
   bandwith of 4
   single 32, 43
business object model 192
business server 7
bytecodes 131-3, 142

C language 50, 78, 145
C++ language 29, 78, 89, 119, 127, 145
cell directory server (CDS) 59
CGI *see* common gateway interface
class concept 84, 150, 153
class identifier 87, 89
client 7, 13, 64
   clone of 99
   connection to server 52
   construction of 50
   identity, verification of 74
client-broker interface 75
client-server architectures 1, 6, 43
   automatic connection 52
   communication structure 51
   Internet and 24
   three-tier application 7-12, 51-7, 203
   two-tier application 26

client stub 14, 46, 53, 71
clipboard 94
clock, machine 60
clone, client 99
code
    application 11, 14
    communication 11, 14
    interface 26
    modification of 16
    reuse of 99
COM see Component Object Model
common gateway interface (CGI) 109
    application server 119
    context files 121
    context saving 120-21
    cookies 121
    hidden fields 120
    between Web server and application
        117
Common Object Request Broker
    Architecture (CORBA) 16-17, 19, 63,
        70, 75, 82, 161
    bridge between DCOM 103
    components of 69
    conceptual model 66
    definitions 69-70
    OLE/COM compared 97, 104
    origin of 65
common object services specification 65
communication 10, 16
    asynchronous 9, 33-5, 37, 64, 72
    bus 1, 4, 9
    client-server model 6, 43
    code 11, 14
    links 2
    one-way 71-2
    point-to-point structure 32
    single bus 32, 43
    structures 5-6, 10, 32, 51
    synchronous 9, 15, 33-4, 37, 53, 64, 71-2,
        181
component-based software 144
Component Object Model (COM) 16, 19,
    78, 81-2
    infrastructure of 87
components 144-5
composite documents 81
    handling of 93, 101-2
composite file management 93
composite objects, management of 95
consistency of transaction 20
containers 92, 95, 144
    Bento 102
context file, concept of 121
contract, concept of 47, 67
control system 22

cookies, concept of 121
CORBA see Common Object Request
        Broker Architecture
CORBA 2.0 standard 75
customization, Java Beans 146
cut-and-paste 94
cyberspace see Internet

data
    distribution of 22
    encoding 51
    notification of modifications to 95
    structure, creation of 190
    uniform transfer of 88, 93-4
data dictionary 178
data formats 11, 38, 51, 98
data object 94
data server 7-8
data transfer 88, 93-4
DCE see distributed computing
        environment
DCE-CIOP 77
DCE RPC 59-60
DCE threads 54, 57-9
DCOM 19, 97
    bridge between CORBA 103
DECmessageQ 9, 36, 38-9
DECnet 33, 38
deferred synchronous communication 71-2,
        75, 181
delete method 114-15
design phase, MethodF 187-93
digital reliable transaction router 22
direct access to data (DAD) 201
diskless node server 57, 62
display control 145
distributed computing environment
        (DCE) 55
    cell 56
    configuration of cell 58
    directory 59
    threads 54, 57-9
distributed file server 57
Distributed Objects Everywhere (DOE) 19,
        77, 97
Distributed Object Management Facility
        (DOMF) 97
distributed processing 63-4
    Java 133
distributed programming tools 57
distributed services 57
distributed systems 28
Distributed Systems Object Model
        (DSOM) 19, 77, 97, 102
distributed time server 57, 60

distributed transaction processing,
  management 40
distribution, unit of 13, 16, 43
DLLs 87, 89
DNS *see* domain name server
document object 95
DOE 19, 77, 97
domain name server (DNS) 59
domain name system 106
DOMF 97
DSOM 19, 77, 97, 102
duration of transaction 20
dynamic data exchange (DDE) 94
dynamic invocation 71-2, 75
dynamic models 179, 183
dynamic relations 16-17

EBCDIC 11, 38, 51
embedding 93, 95
encapsulation 16, 63, 151
entity types 175
environment handling 23
event diagram 179-81
event management 145
event notification 78
Excel 101
external data representation (XDR) 51
external object 92

file, structure of 101
file management system 93
file servers 109, 118
fileset 61
File Transfer Protocol (FTP) 107
  HTTP compared 116
firewall 116, 129
forms, HTML 114-15
Forté 202
FTP *see* File Transfer Protocol

garbage collector 139
get method 114-15
GetContect(url) instruction 138
GetData 83
GIF images 109, 112
GIOP/IIOP 77
global directory server (GDS) 59
global naming system 39
globally unique identifier (GUID) 83-4
Gopher 107
graphical user interface 7-8
group type 194
GUID 83-4

hidden field, concept of 120
HTML *see* Hypertext Markup Language
HTTP *see* Hypertext Transfer Protocol
hyperlinks 108, 110-13
hypermedia document 108
Hypertext Markup Language (HTML) 25,
  109-10
  document 108, 110-12
  forms 114-15
  images in document 113
  link 111-2
Hypertext Transfer Protocol (HTTP) 25,
  107, 114, 109
  File Transfer Protocol compared 116
  security 116-17

IAdviseSink interface 95
icons, as links 112
IDataObject interface 94
IDL *see* Interface Definition Language
IIOP 127
images 112-3
implementation association 196
implementation database 74
implementation model, MethodF 193-9
  associations used in 195-6
  example of 198
  types used in 194-5
implementation phase, MethodF 193-9
implementation type 194
independence of transaction 20
inheritance 17-18, 63, 99, 154-5
  aggregation compared 160
  instance generation compared 156
  multiple 99
input parameters 49, 53, 193
input queue 33-6
input stream 117
input-output parameters 49, 193
instance, concept of 150, 153
interaction diagram 179
interactive link, analysis model 176
interface 6, 13, 17, 32, 43
  access to an object's 84
  characteristics of 84
  code 26
  concept of 67, 82
  instance 82
  methods 82
  model 184
  object type 174-5, 178
  operations 82
  publication and discovery of 145
Interface Definition Language (IDL) 14-15,
  17, 50, 187

internal object 92
Internet 24, 105
    address 105
    architectures 118
    client-server model and 24
    downloading an application 135
    protocols 107-8
    putting applications on 122-3
    service providers 105
    use of middleware 125
Internet Inter-Orb Protocol (IIOP) 127
Interpreter module, JVM 137-8
interrupt processing 6
interviewer/interviewee model 6
Intranet 107, 128
introspection 146
invocation
    dynamic 71-2, 75
    of methods 74
    static 71
IP address 105
IUnknown interface 85-6, 92

Java 127-8, 131
    applets 127, 132-3, 135-44
    construction of client and server objects
        141
    language 131
    use phases of 132
Java Beans 144, 146
    ActiveX compared 147-8
Java RMI 140
Java Virtual Machine (JVM) 132-9
    structure of 138
javac command 141, 143
Just-in-Time (JIT) compiler 139

Kerberos 40, 60

LAN 22, 55, 105
libraries 73, 87
    JVM 139
life cycle 78
linking 95
links 161
    dynamic 183
    static 183
little-endian 51-2
load balancing 20, 22
Loader module, JVM 137
local area network (LAN) 22, 55, 105
local file system (LFS) 61

machine naming 105
    rules on structure 106
many-to-many relations 162
many-to-one communications 10
marshalling 51, 98, 140
master entity 43
master-slave model 37
memory management 87-8
message
    asynchronous transmission of 9
    backing up of 35
    broadcasting of 10, 36
    guaranteed delivery of 9, 22, 35
    handling of 36
    queues 11-12, 31-4
    selective reading of 10
    self-describing 12, 39
    size of 12, 39
    structure of 36-8
    synchronous transmission of 9
    transmission of 9, 16
message-based middleware 31
    guarantee of delivery 35
    waiting queues 9-11, 31
MethodF 28, 165
    analysis phase 173-86
    design phase 187-93
    implementation phase 193-9
    origins of 165-6
    phases of 167
    specification phase 167-73
methods, invocation of 74
middleware 1, 4, 9
    choosing 11, 202
    limitations of 20
    message-based 9-11, 31, 35
    message queue 37-9
    object-oriented 16-19, 27-29
    positioning of 5
    remote procedure calls 13-16
modelling 16
MOMA 12
MPEG standard 109
moniker, object 88, 93
MQSeries 9, 39-40
MS-Word 95, 101, 112
multi-reader queues 39
multi-threading 23, 36
multiple access 79

name
    object 17
    servers 23, 52, 54, 57, 59-60, 140, 142-4
    system 12
    use of 5

naming
      diagram 183
      machine 105-6
      managing 88
      new objects 88
native methods 139
navigator *see* browser
network data representation (NDR) 51
network protocols 6, 9, 25, 33, 41, 107

object
      abstraction of 154
      adapter 73-75
      attributes 149
      Bento container 102
      concept of 83, 149
      container 92, 95
      encapsulation of 151-2
      external 92
      implementation of 91
      internal 92
      name 78, 149
      operations 149
      reuse of 91-2
      type 153, 187-91, 194
object-based analysis model 174
      construction stages 17
      links used in 176
      viewports on objects 174
object-based middleware *see* object-
      oriented middleware
ObjectBroker 19, 77, 97, 103
Object Data Base Connectivity (ODBC) 133
object generator 192
object licences, management of 79
object management architecture (OMA)
      65, 78
object middleware 17
Object Modelling Technique (OMT) 29,
      155, 160, 165
object-oriented analysis 165
object-oriented database adapter 73
object-oriented middleware 16-19, 27-29,
      81
Object-Oriented Software Engineering
      (OOSE) 28, 165
object references, generation of 74
object request broker (ORB) 17, 63, 65
      interface 75
object services 65
object technology 16, 63, 149
      phases of 153
      principal characteristics of 151-2
object types 153, 194
      design of 187

design by inheritance 188-9
design by delegation 190
location of 191
obtained by link, analysis model 176
OLE/COM 81, 161
      CORBA compared 97, 104
OLE2 81, 92-6
OLTP 21-2
OMA 65, 78
OMG IDL 67
OMG 19, 65, 77-8, 97
OMT 29, 155, 160, 165
one-to-many communications 10, 16
one-to-one communications 16
one-way communications 71-2
OOSE 28, 165
OpenDoc 101-2
Open Software Foundation (OSF) 54
OpenVMS 22
operations, object 17, 149
      encapsulation and 152
ORB *see* object request broker
Orbix 97
ORBPlus 19, 77
OSF IDL RPC 48
OSF/DCE 16, 23
OSF 54
OSI model 5, 32-3
output parameters 49, 53, 193
output queue 33-6
overloading concept 157

p-code 131
packaging, Java Beans 146
page_i/f 124, 127
PDO 97
peer-peer communications 37
PERL 119
persistence service 78, 145-6
persistent call 181
platforms 10
plug-and-play 63
point-to-point communications
      structure 31
      inter-application 33
Point-to-Point Protocol (PPP) 107
pointers 82-4, 131
polymorphism technique 158-9
portability, concept of 127, 131
post method 114-15
PostScript 111
PowerPoint 95
procedure, concept of 14-15
procedure calls 44
      types of 181

processing server 7-8, 26
protocols 6, 9, 25, 33, 41, 107
proxy object 90, 98
proxy server 116
put method 114-15

Queues 11-12, 31-4
QueryInterface function 85-7, 92
QUERY_STRING variable 117-18

RAMS 168-9
rapid application development 1
recovery, data 20
reference link 196
referenced by link, analysis model 176
Registry entity 140, 142-4
relational service 78-9
Release function 85-7, 92
remote method invocation 140
    execution of 143
remote procedure calls 13-16, 44, 63, 88
    client 46
    components of 47
    concept of contract 47
    principles of 46
    server 46
remote reference layer 140
Requirement Analysis for Management
    Systems (RAMS) 168-9
residence association 195
resource handling 20
root class 99-100
root object 94
RPC *see* remote procedure calls
RPC-based middleware 43

scripts 145
search tools 117-8
security 60-1, 79
security server 57, 60-1
selective read 36
self-describing messages 39
Serial Line Internet Protocol (SLIP) 107
serialization technique 140
server 7, 13, 64
    connection to client 52
    construction of 50
    different types of 89
    machine 56-7
    starting and stopping 74
    structure of 68
server adapter 73
server-broker interface 75

service control manager (SCM) 87
server location service 87
server stub 14, 46, 53, 71
SetData 83
shared instances 197
single communications bus 32
skeleton 71, 75, 99
slave entity 43
Smalltalk 78
SNA 33
SOM 102
specification phase, MethodF 167-73
state transition diagram 181-2
static invocation 71
static model 183
static relations 16-17, 154
STDL standard 23
streams 93
stub/skeleton layer 140
stubs 14, 75, 90, 99
sub-types 155-61
super-types 155-6
synchronous communication 9, 15, 33-4,
        37, 53, 64, 71-2, 181
    deferred 71-2, 75
    with timeouts 181
system failure 4, 20, 22, 61
System Object Model (SOM) 102

TCL 119
TCP 55
TCP/IP 25, 33, 77
Telnet 107
threads, DCE 54, 57-9
three-tier model 7-9, 25-7
time, concept of 60
TopEnd 40
tracing facilities 22
transaction 5, 15, 20, 23, 78-9
    characteristics of 20, 78
    handling 20
transaction monitor 20-4
transfer, reliability of 4, 15
transport layer 140
two-tier application 26
type, object 153, 194

UDP *see* user datagram protocol
uni-directional call 181
uniform resource characteristics (URC)
        110
uniform resource locator (URL) 109, 117,
        119
    conection 138

uniform resource name (URN) 110
universal time co-ordinated (UTC) 60
universal unique identifier (uuid) 48, 60
UNIX 10, 22, 81
URC *see* uniform resource characteristics
URL *see* uniform resource locator
URN *see* uniform resource name
use case 165, 170-3, 179
   description of 172
   example of 172
user datagram protocol (UDP) 55
user interface 7-8
user machine 56
uuid 48, 60

VAX 22
verifier, JVM 138
viewports 174
virtual private network 128

waiting-oriented middleware 32
WAN 22, 55
Web application
   generic architecture of 124
   integration of 123-8
   integrating with object-based
     middleware 126
   using intelligent clients 127
Web browser 108
Web clients 108, 110
Web server 25, 26, 108-9, 116
Wide Area Information Service (WAIS)
   107
wide area network (WAN) 22, 55
Windows-NT 10, 22, 81
World Wide Web (WWW) 24, 105, 107-16
   hyperlinks 108, 110-13
   see also under Web
wrapping technique 123
WWW *see* World Wide Web